MY FIRST AUTUMN

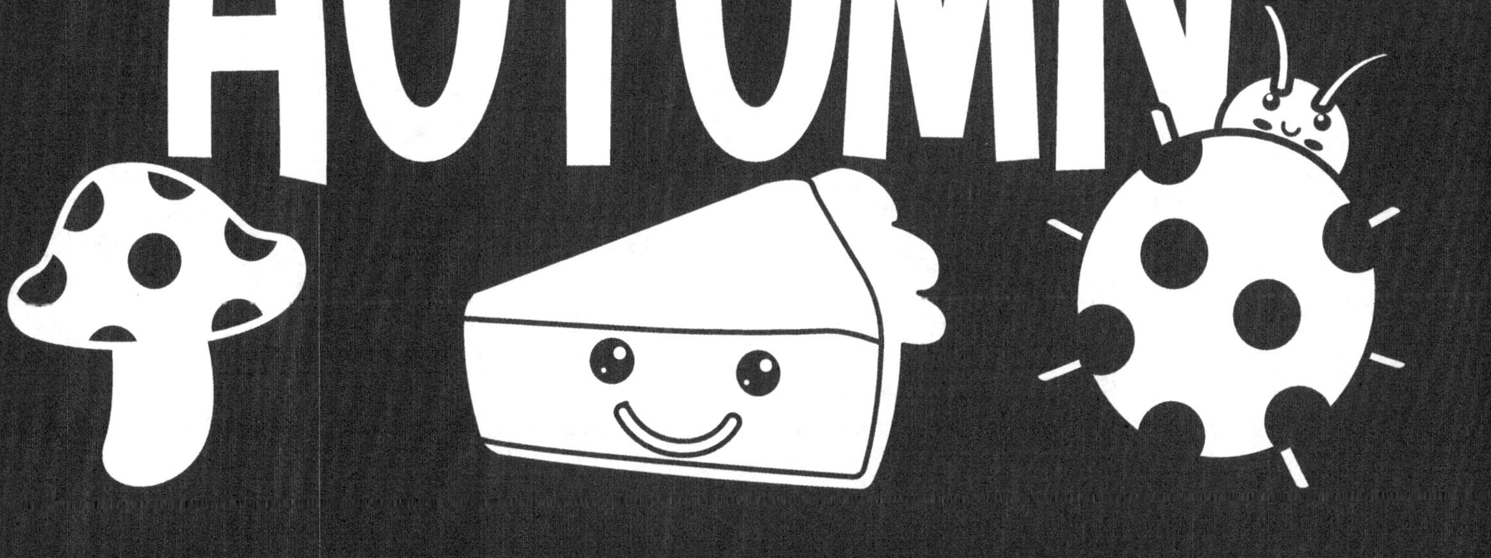

BABY NAME

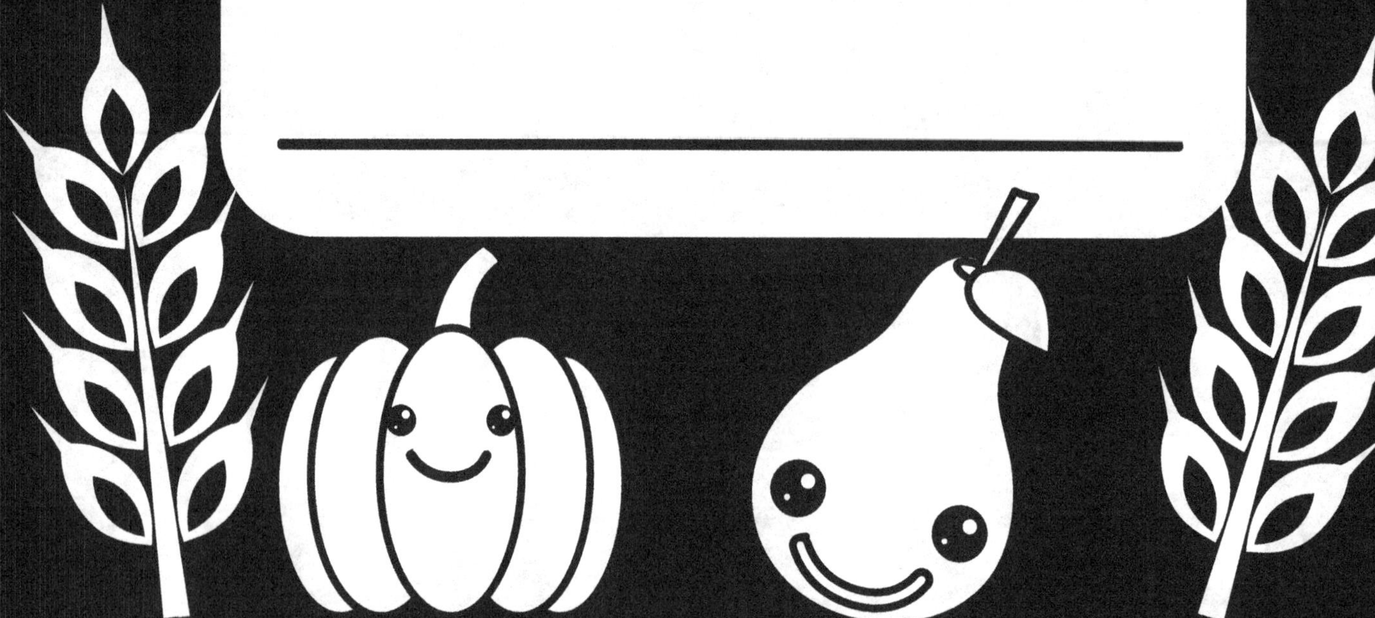

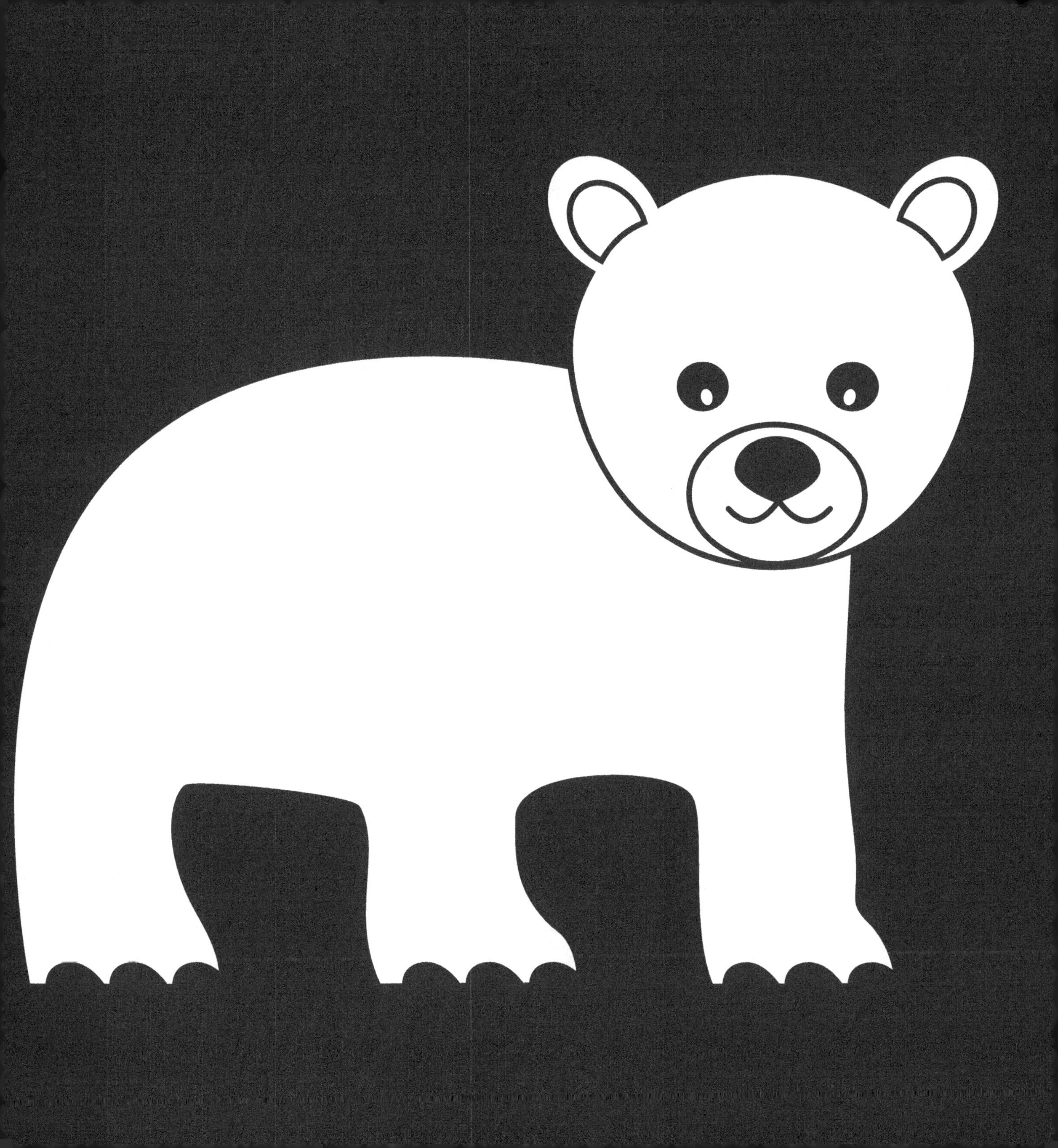

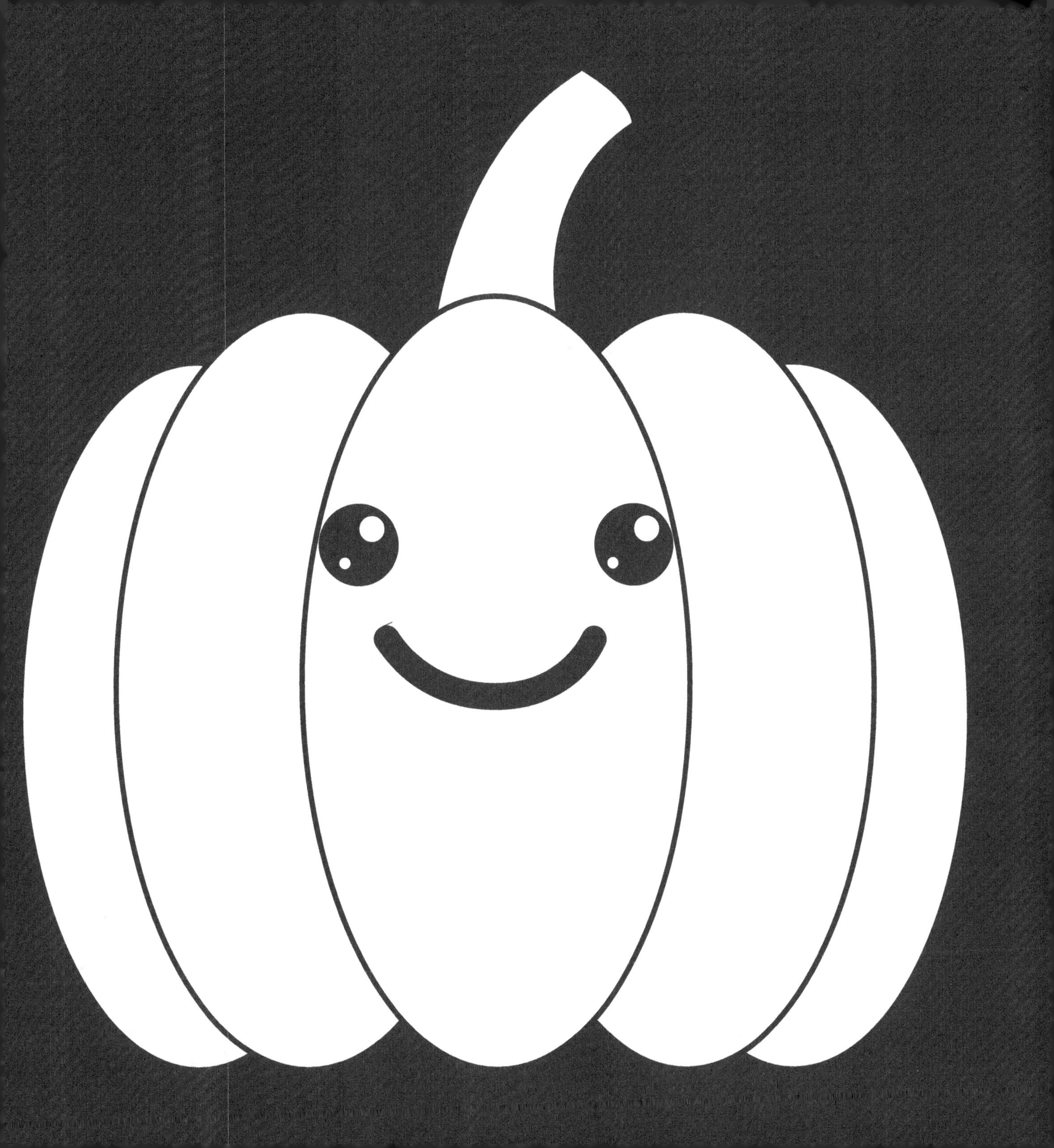

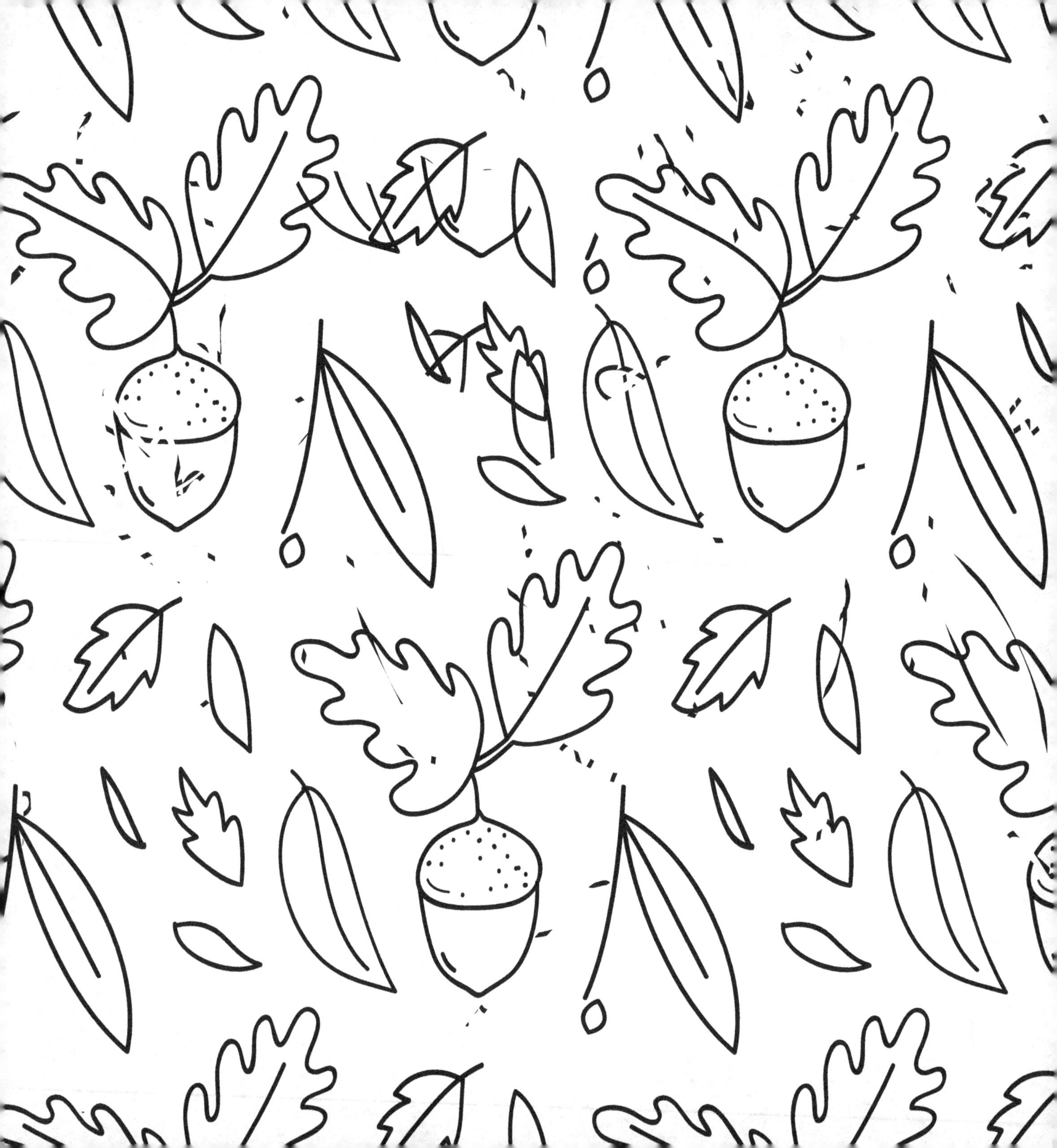

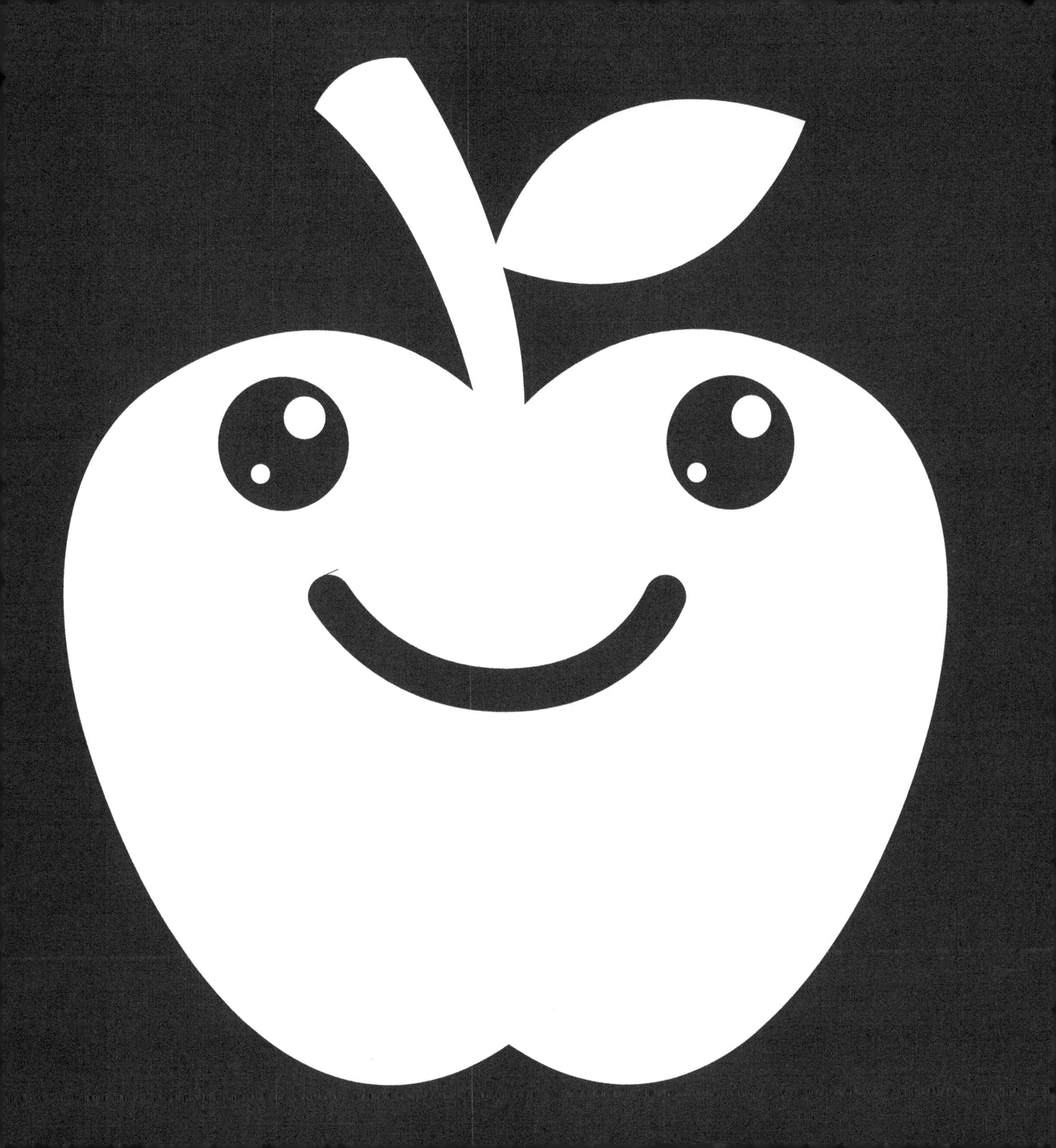

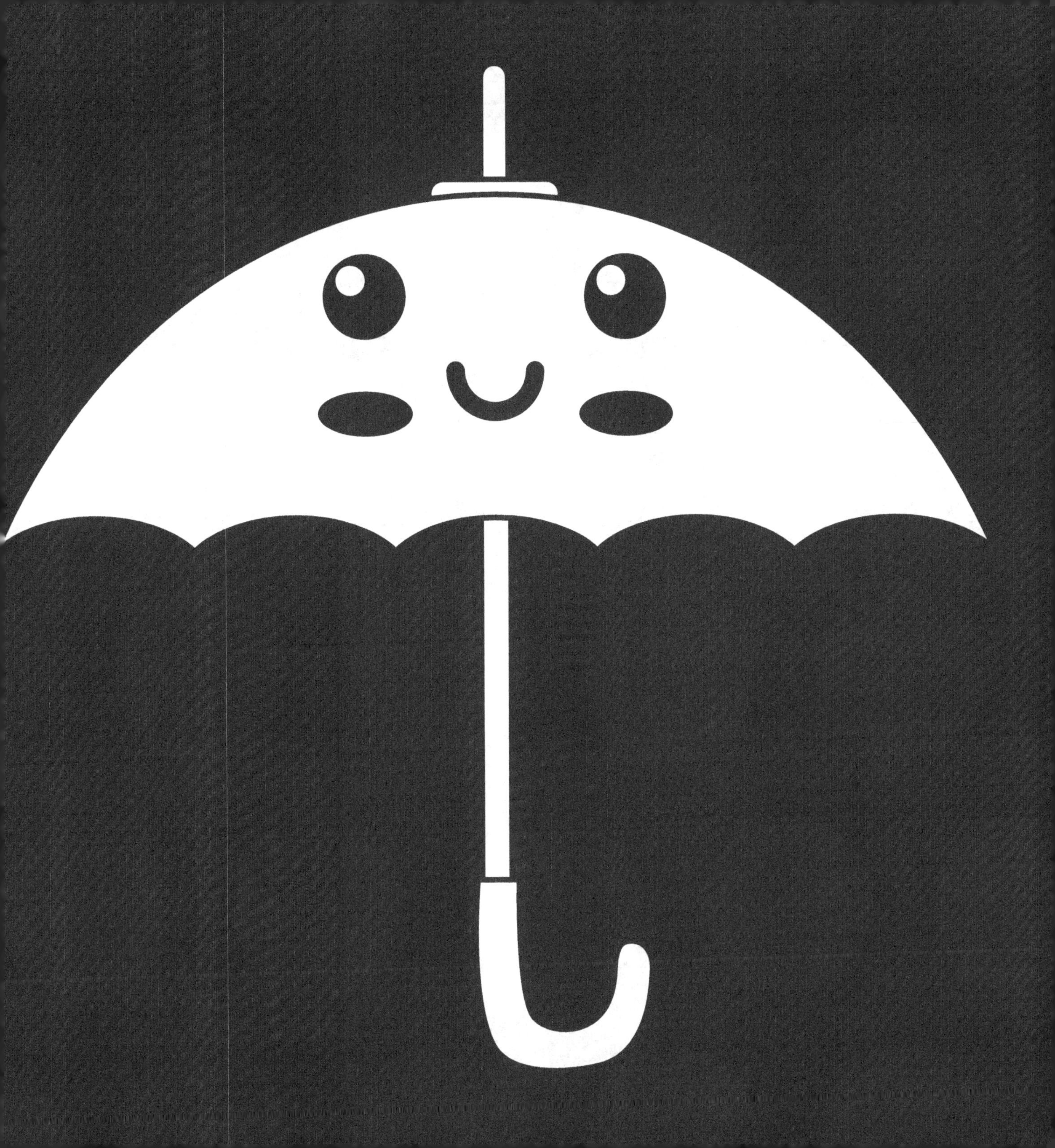

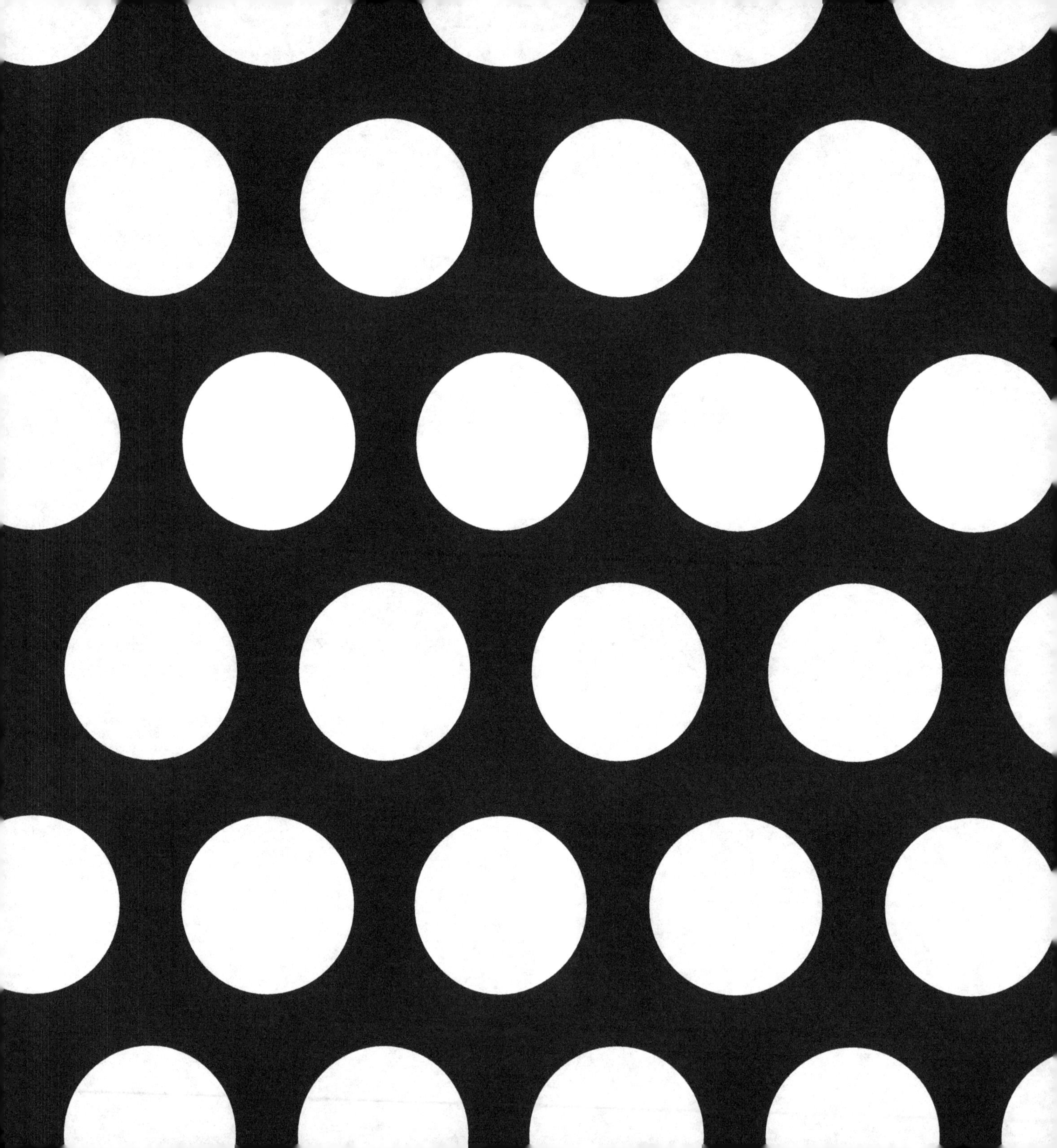

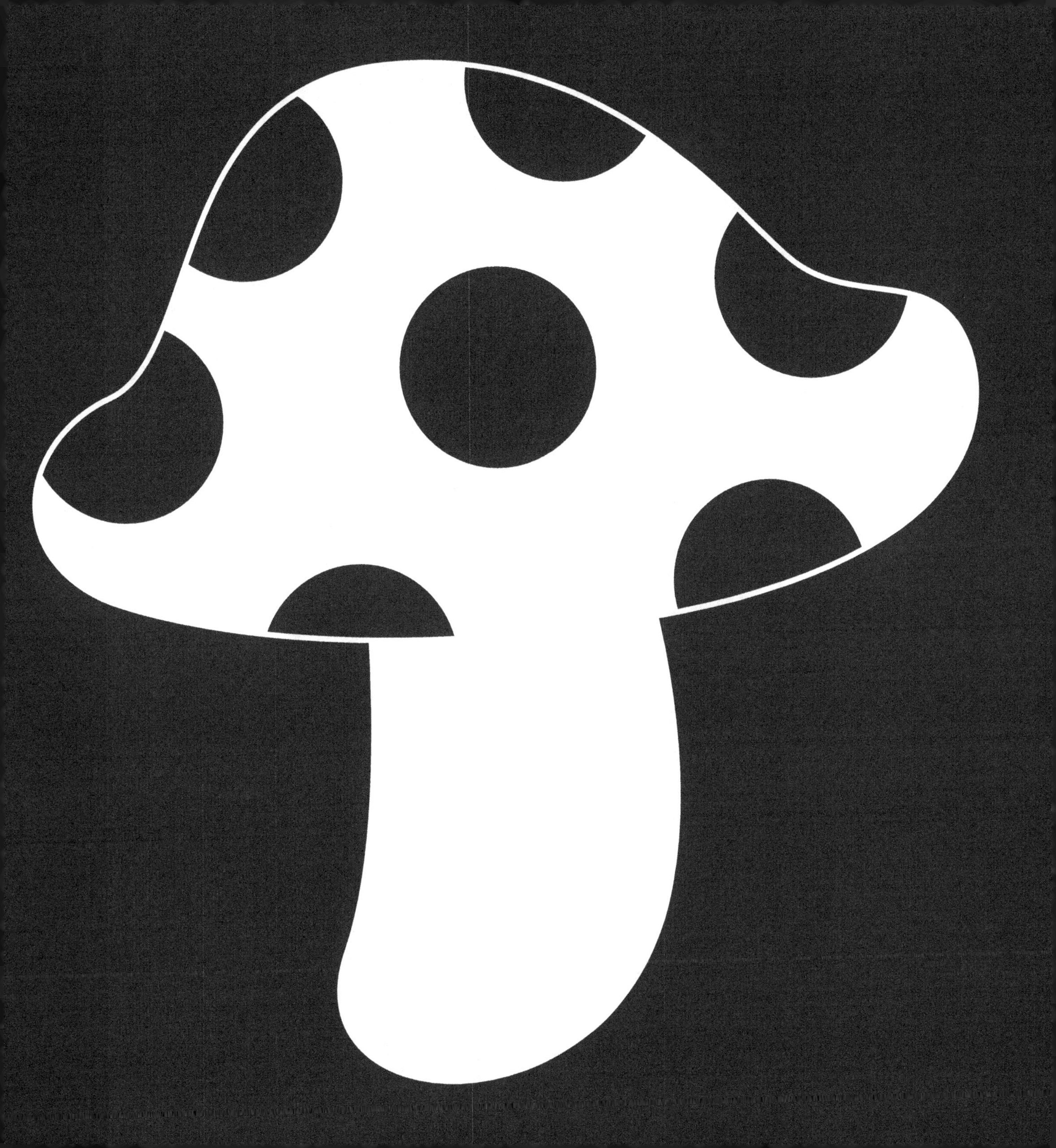

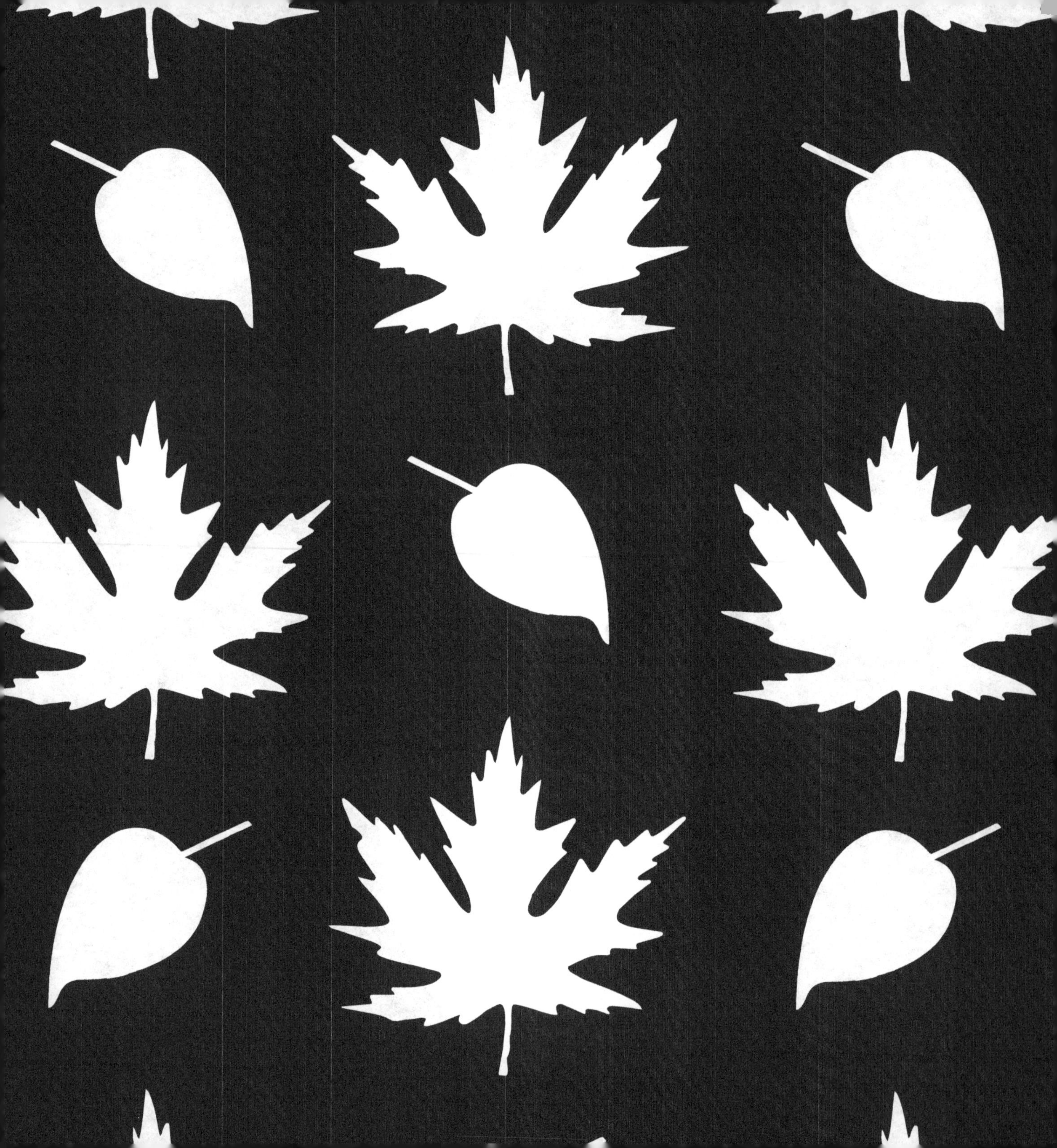

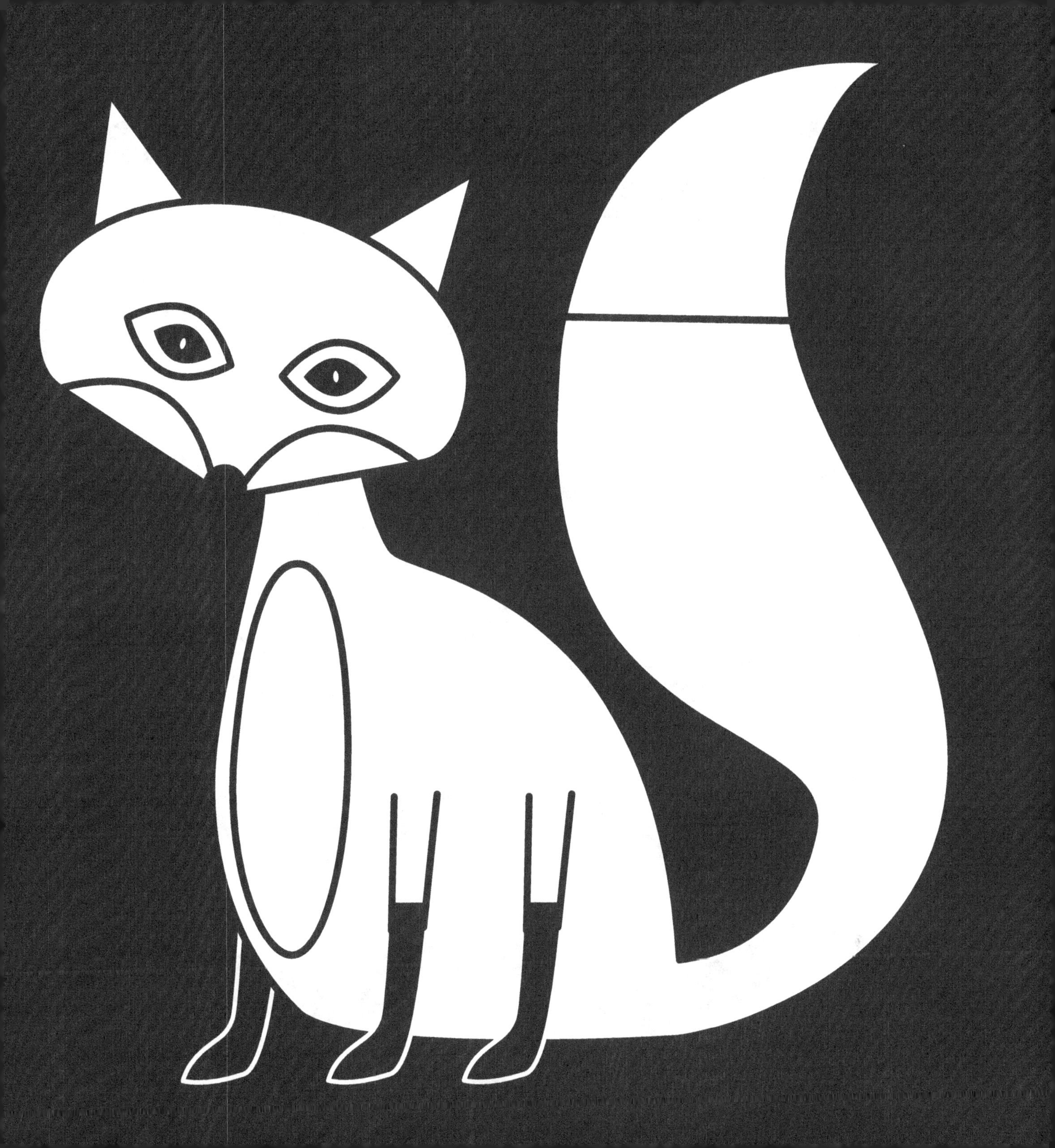

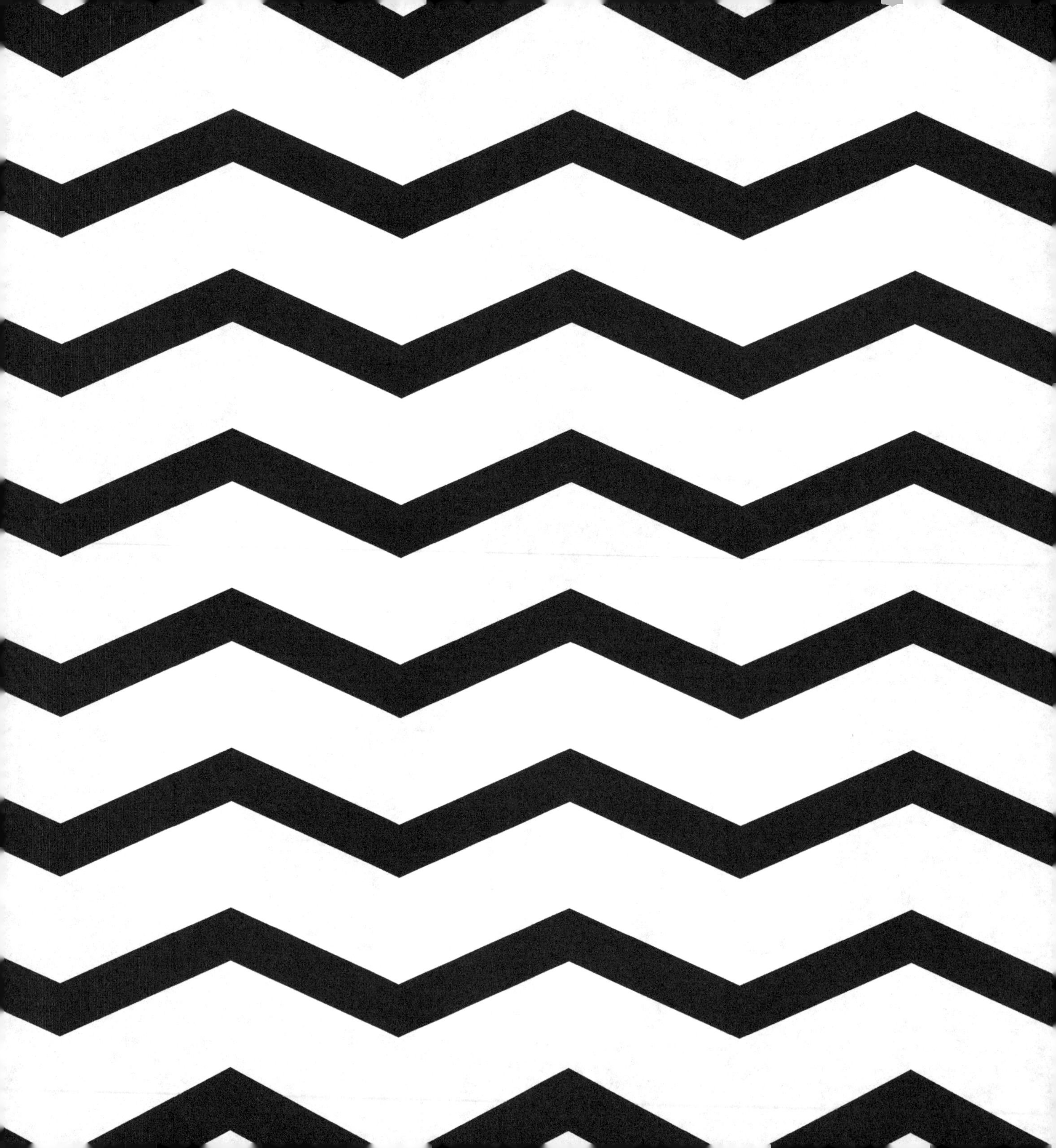

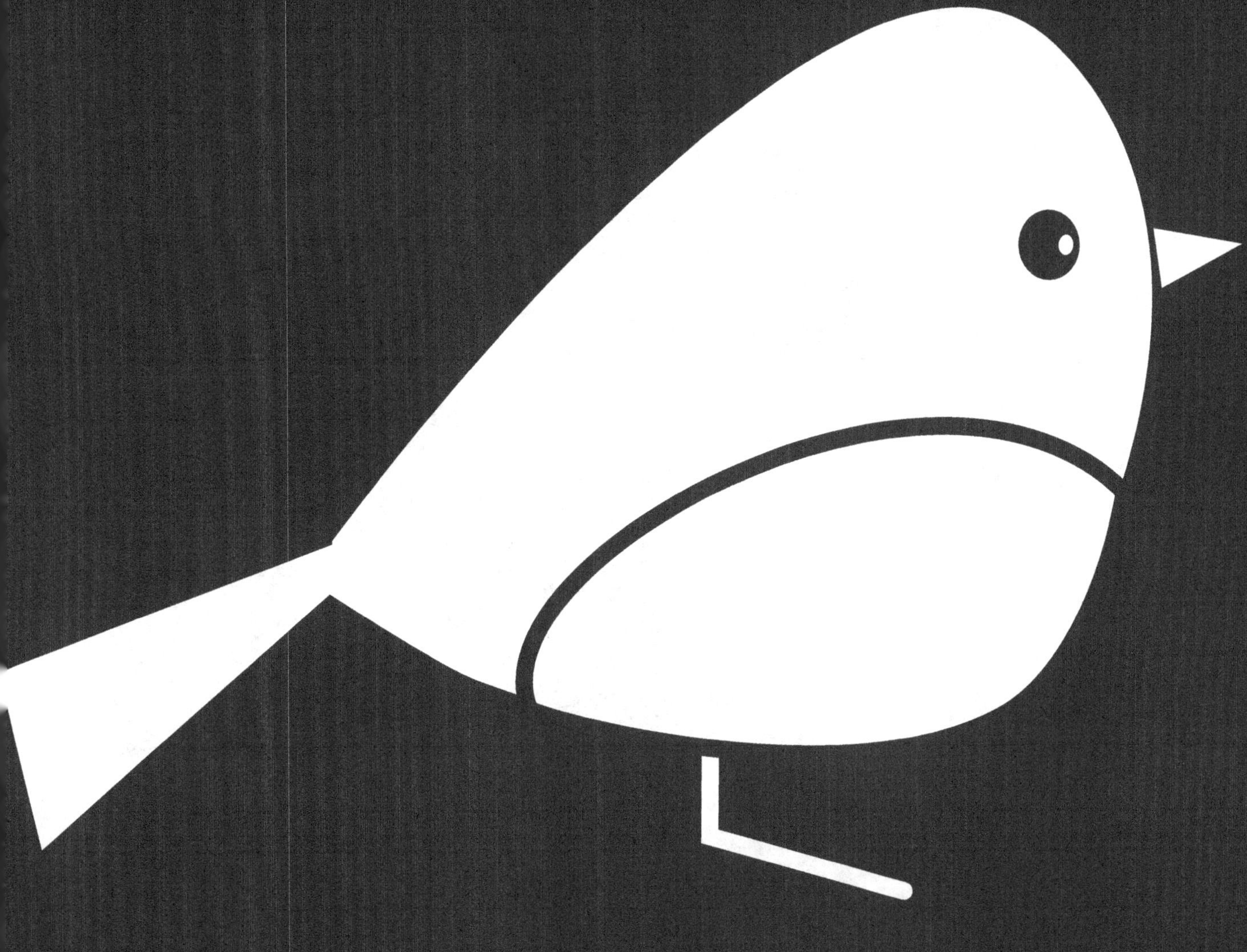

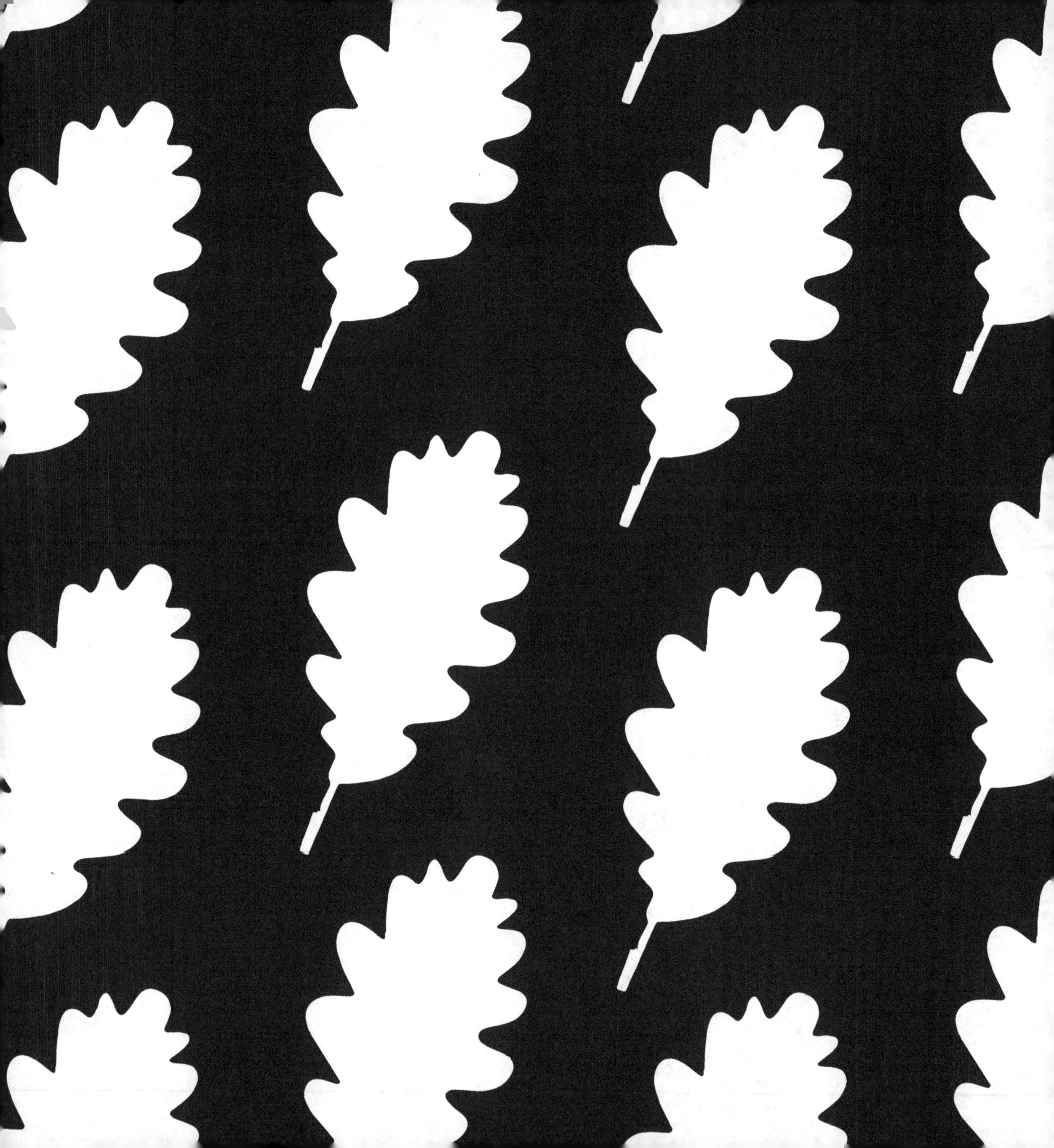

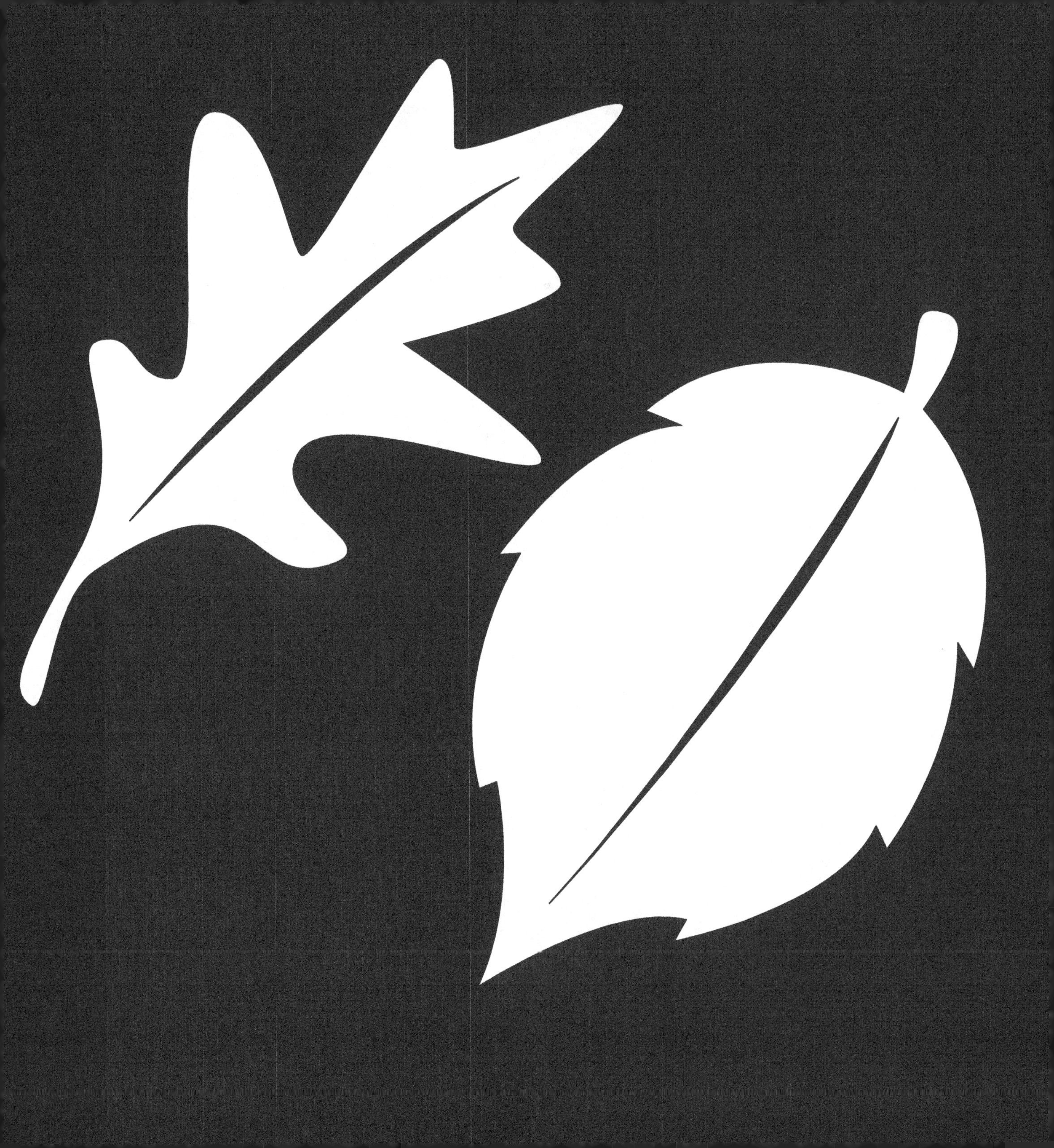

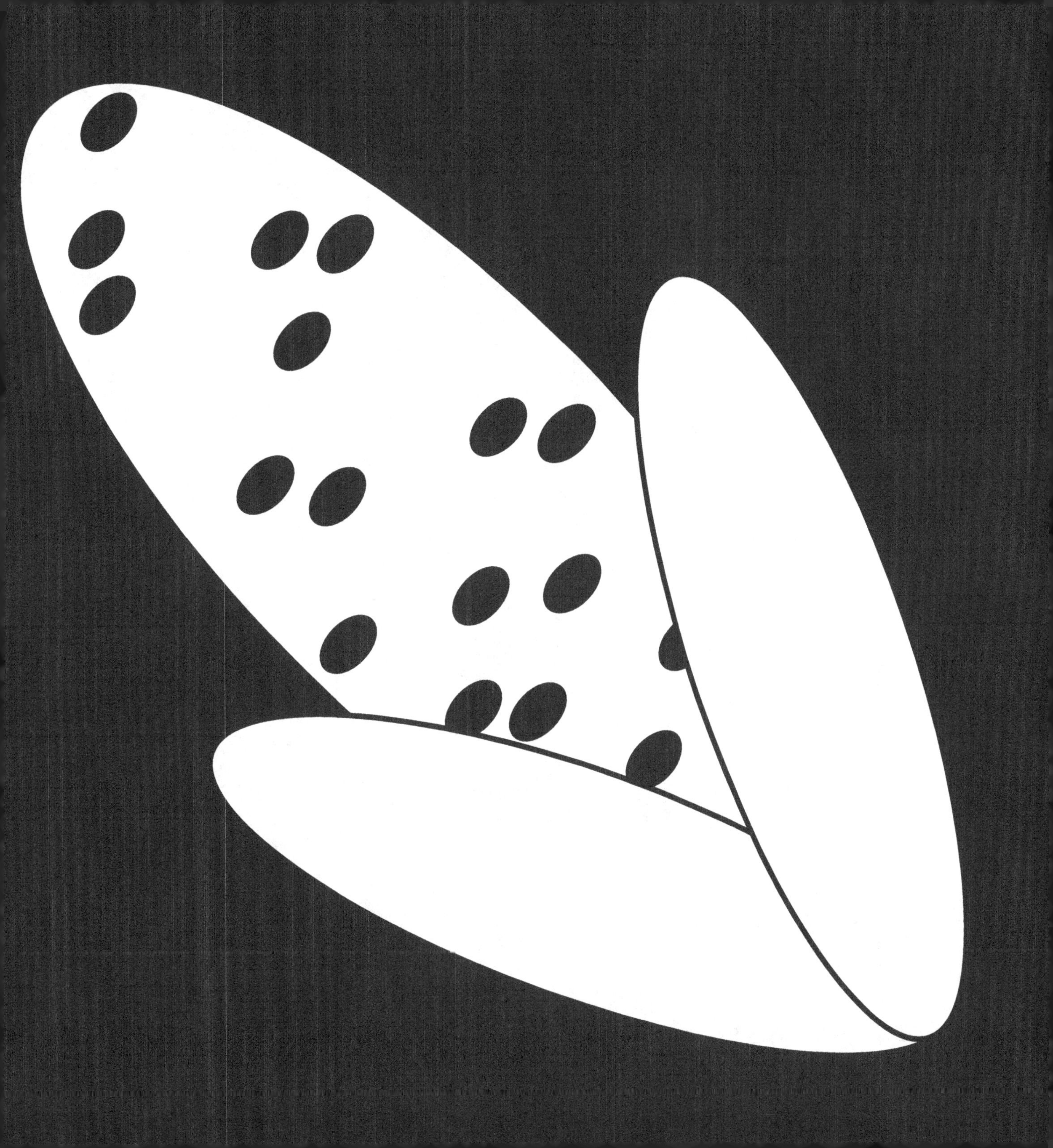

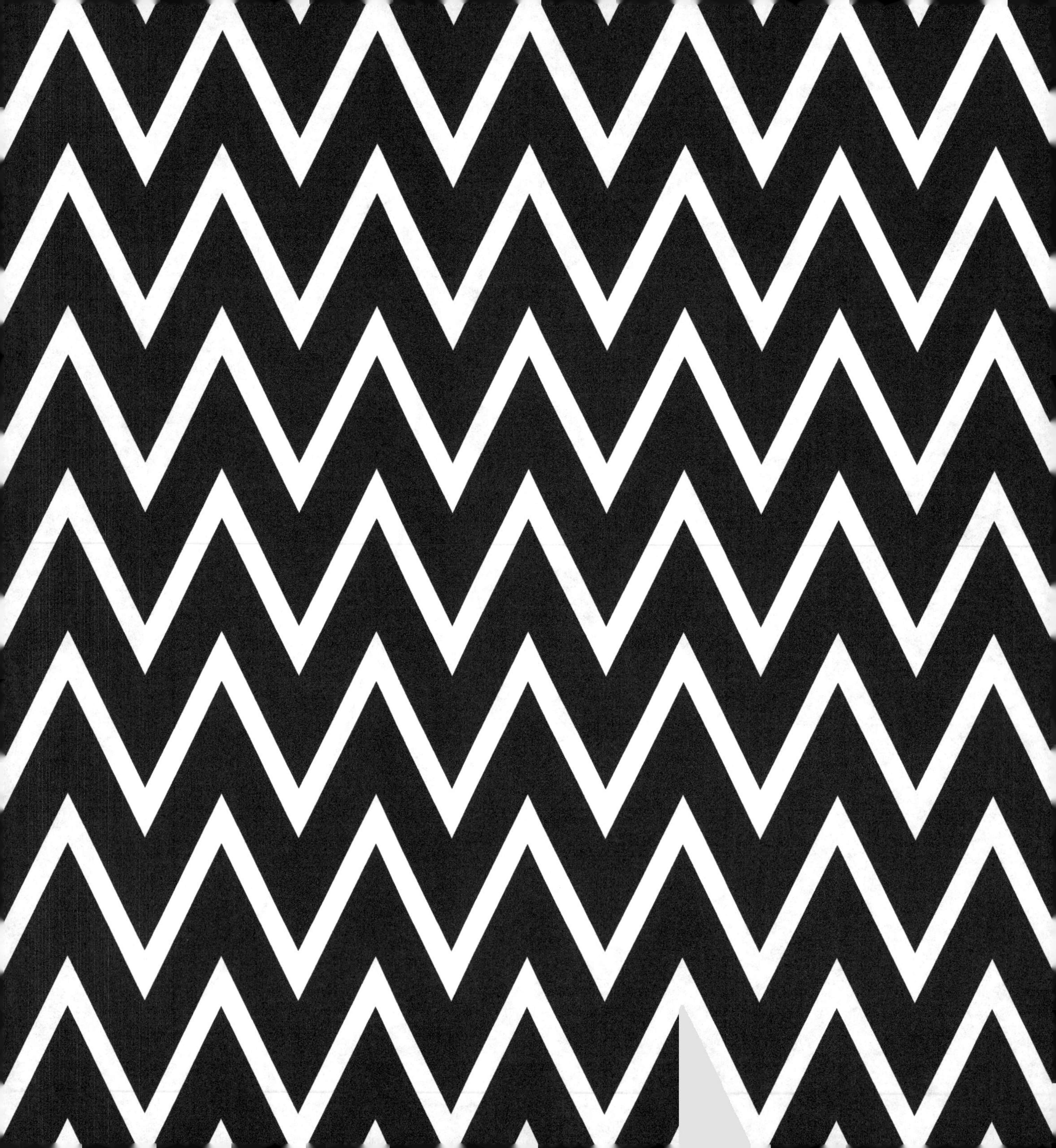

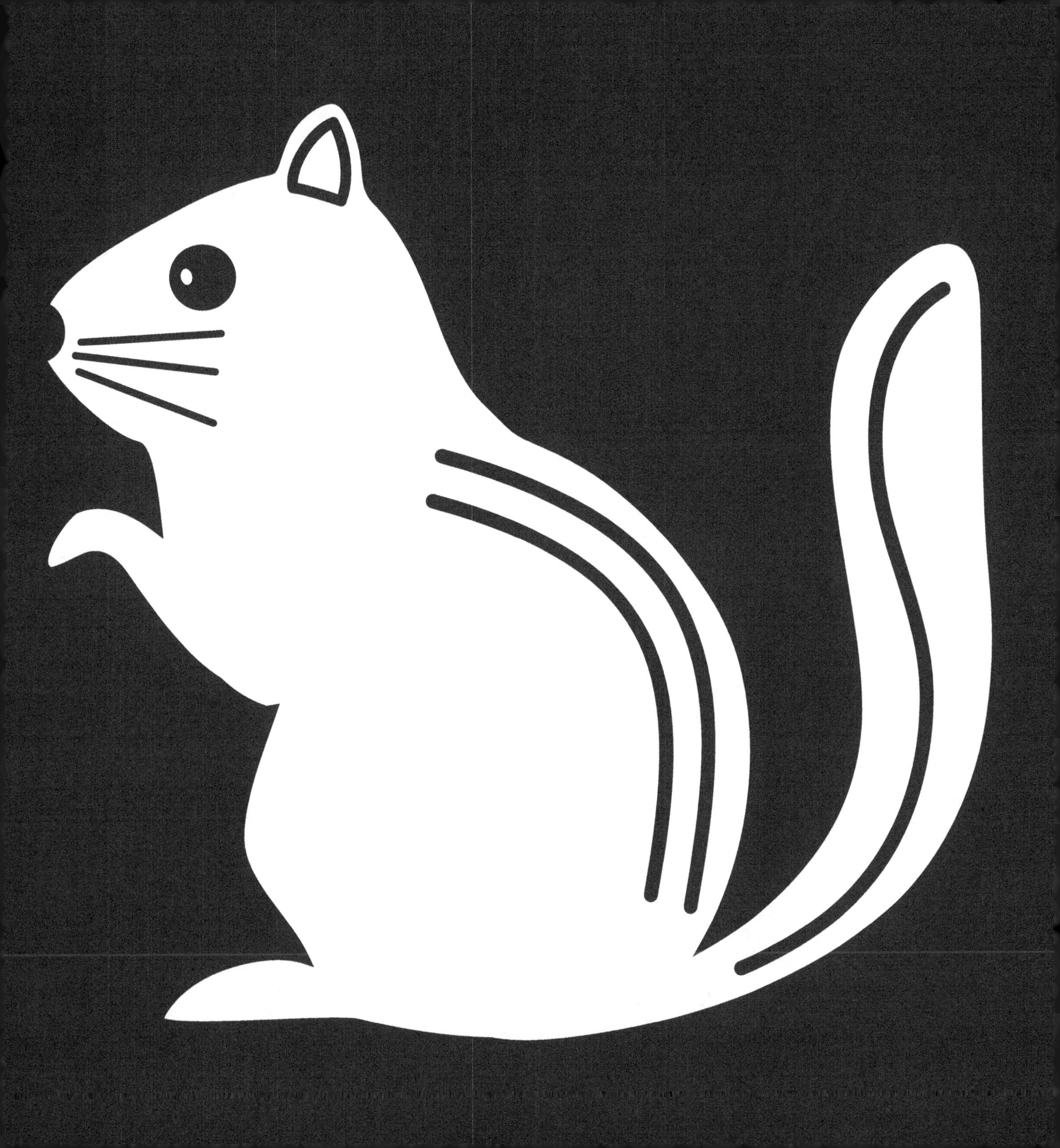

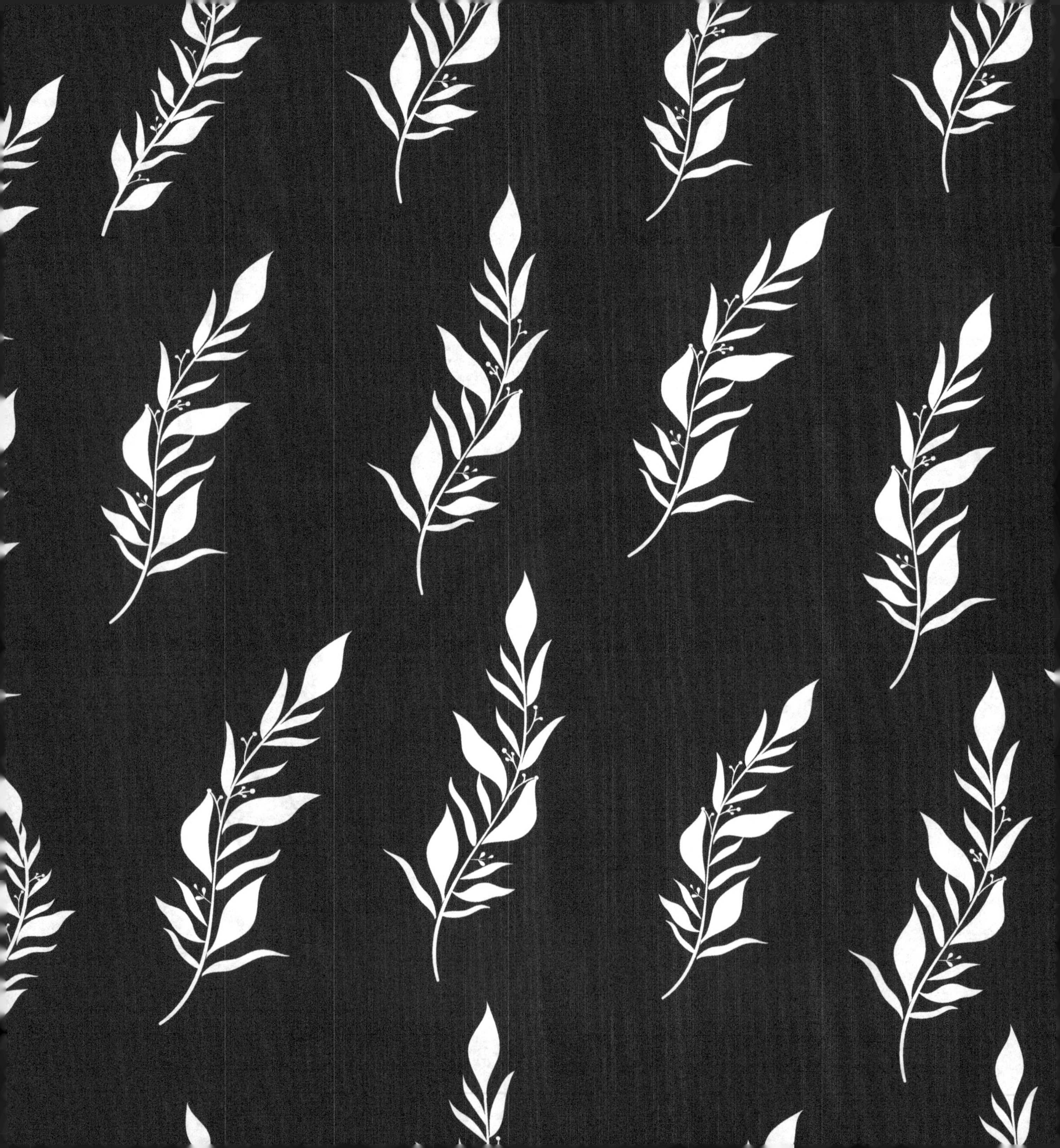

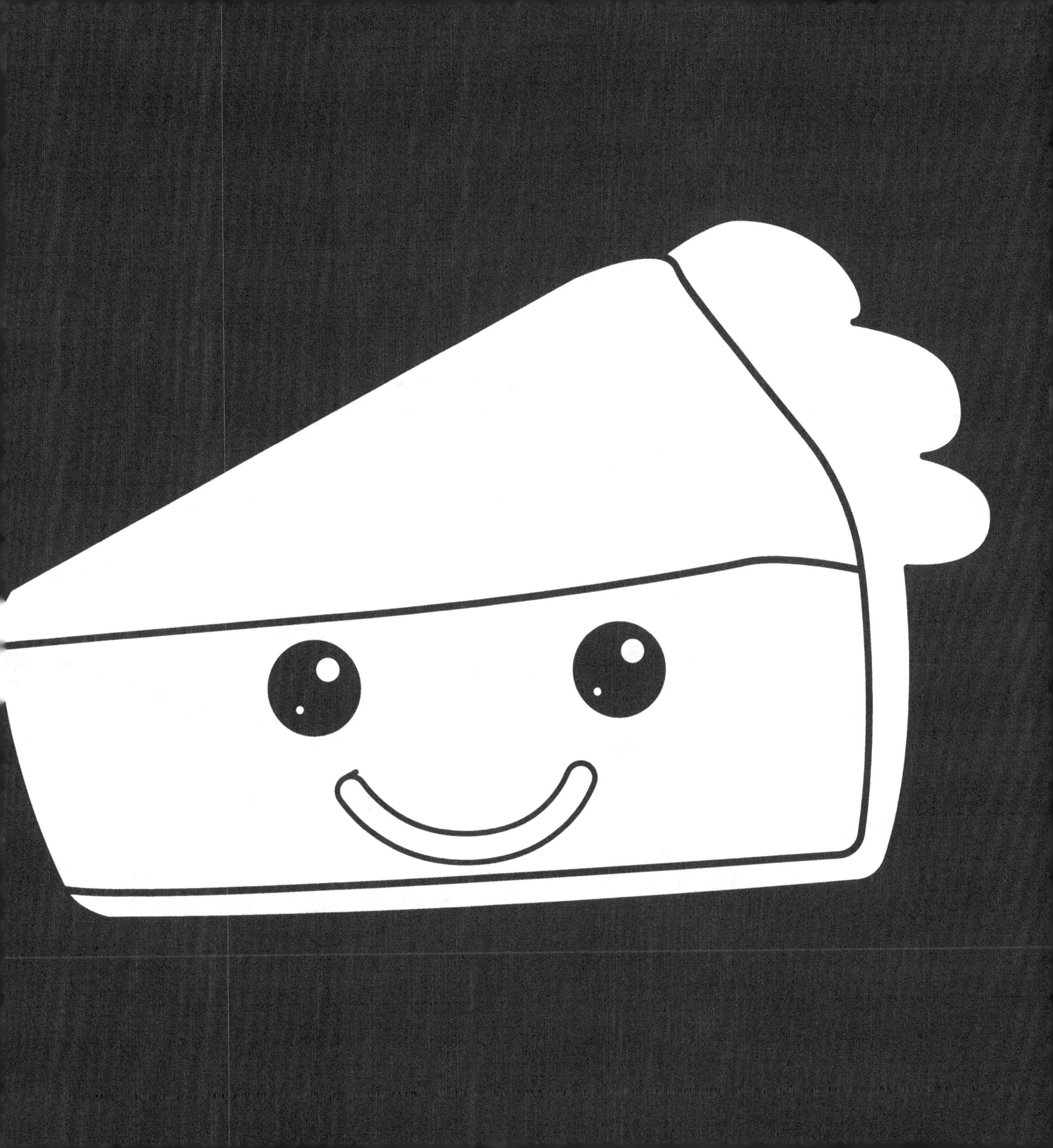

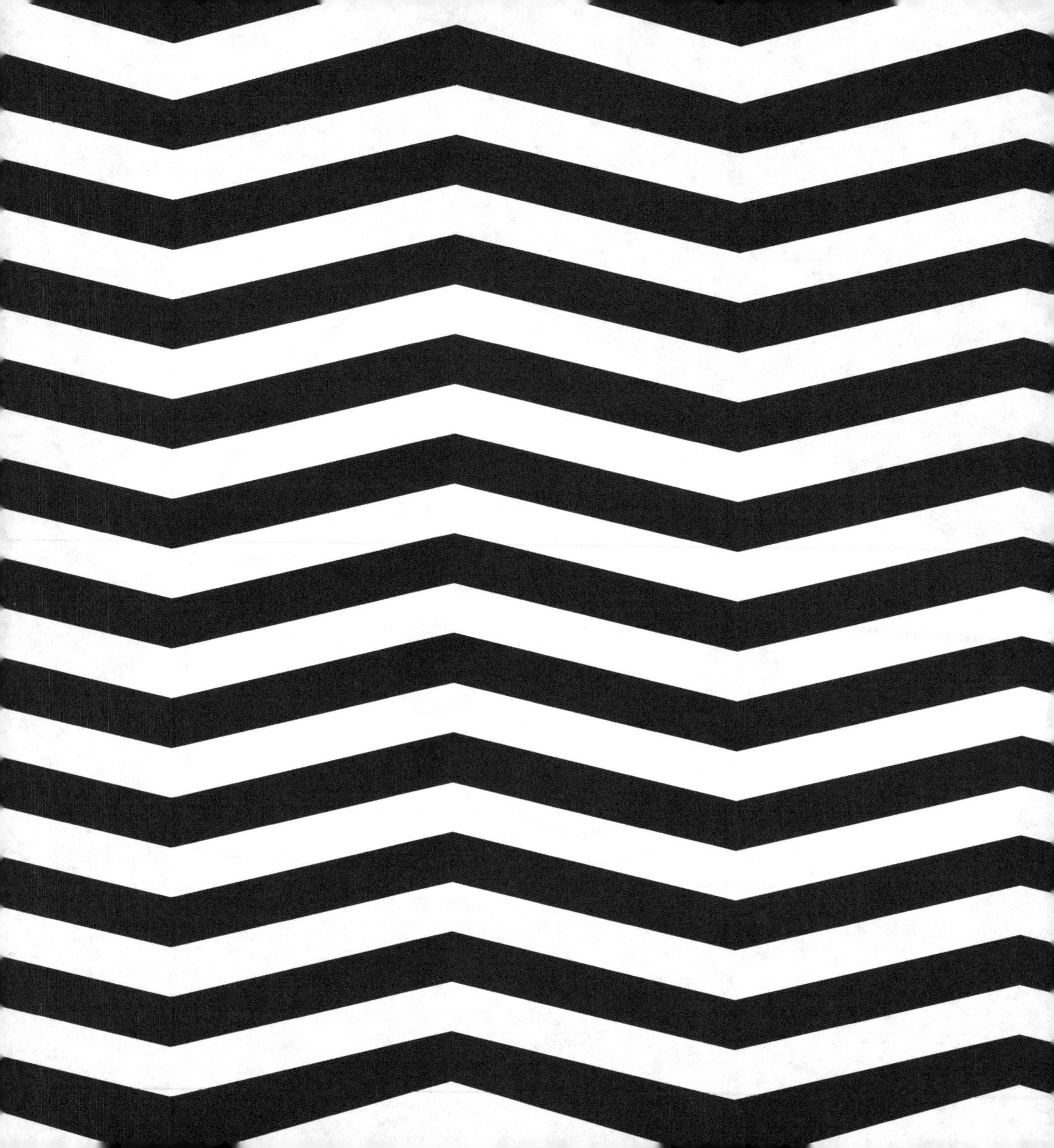

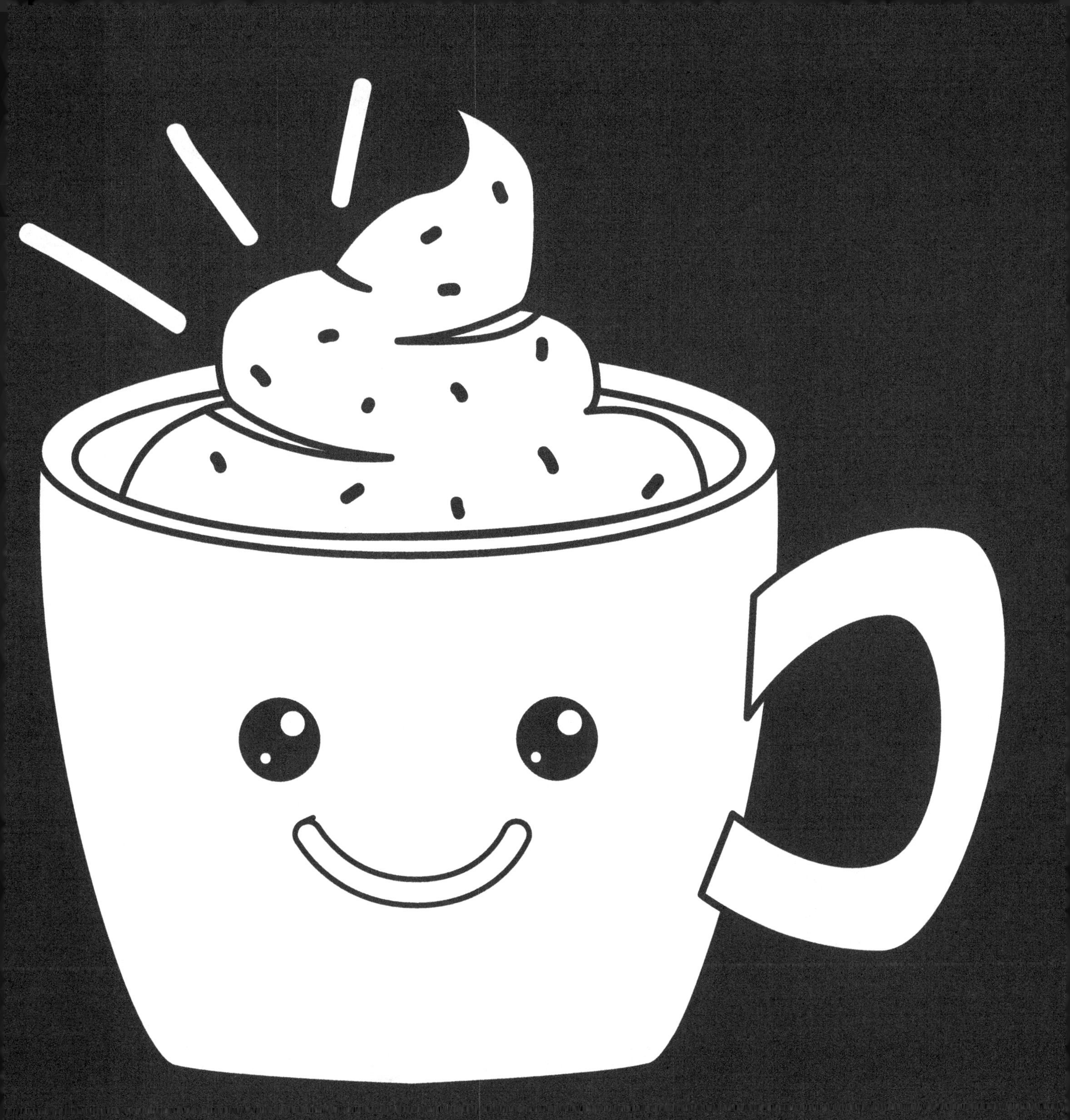

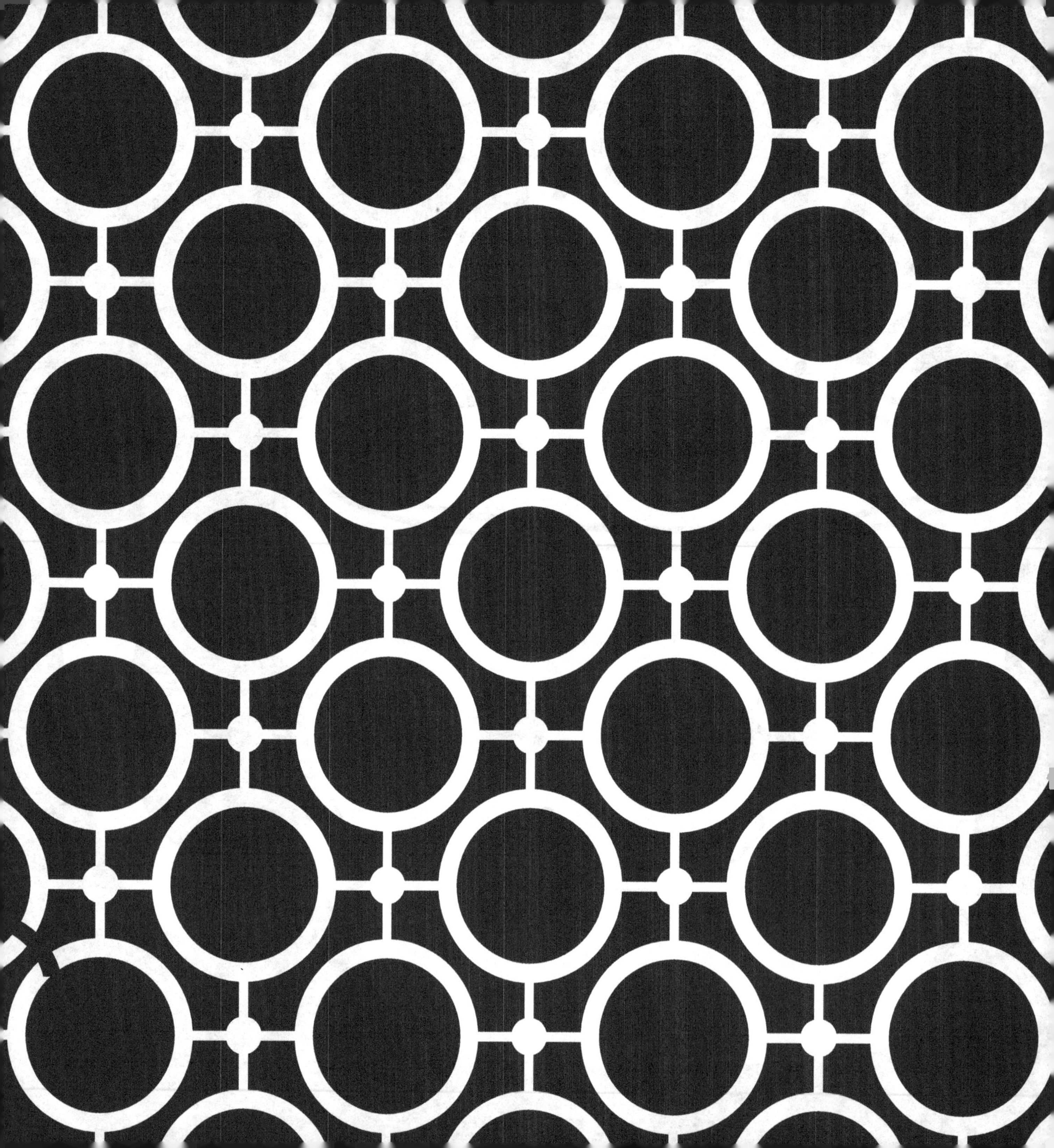

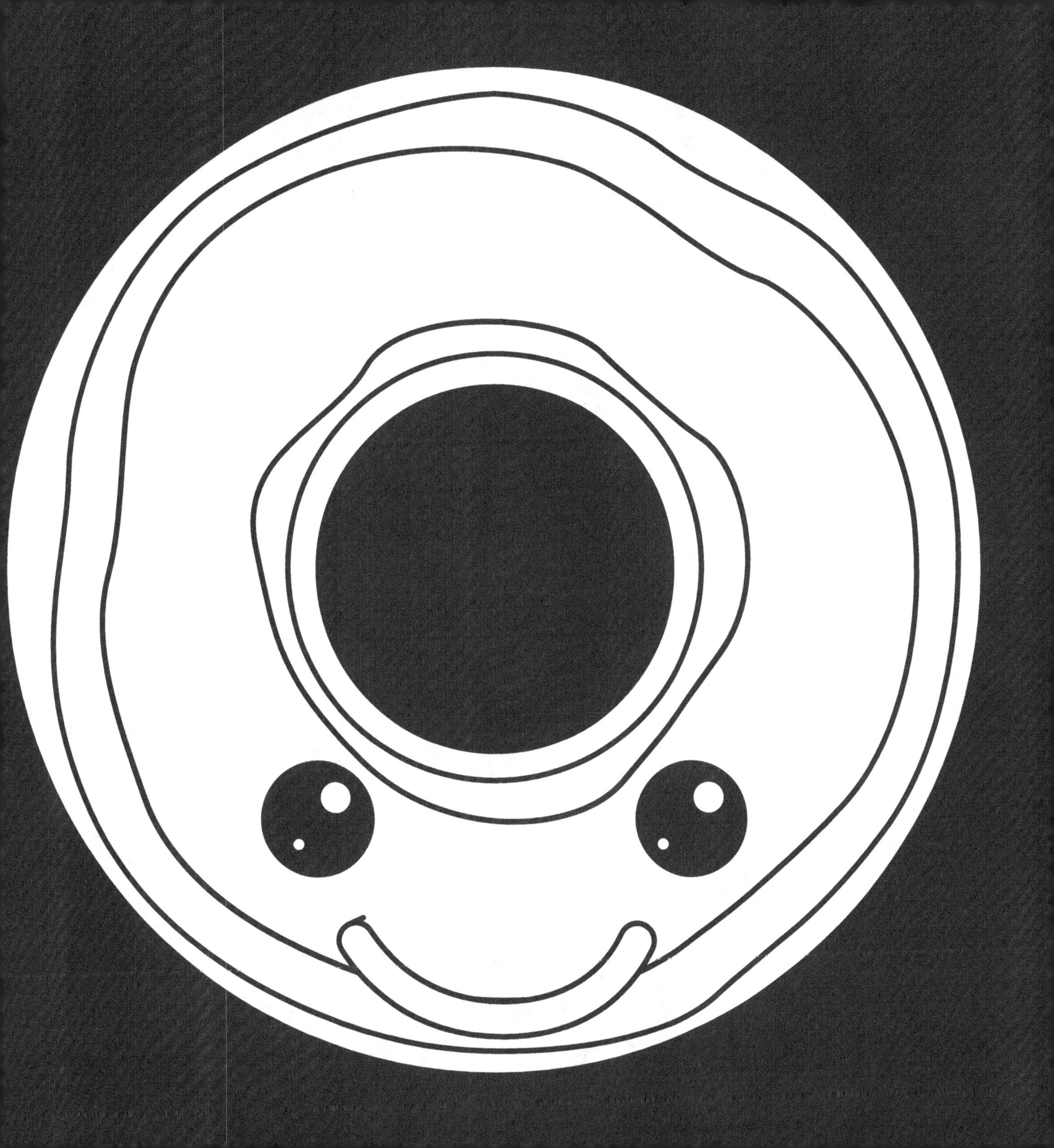

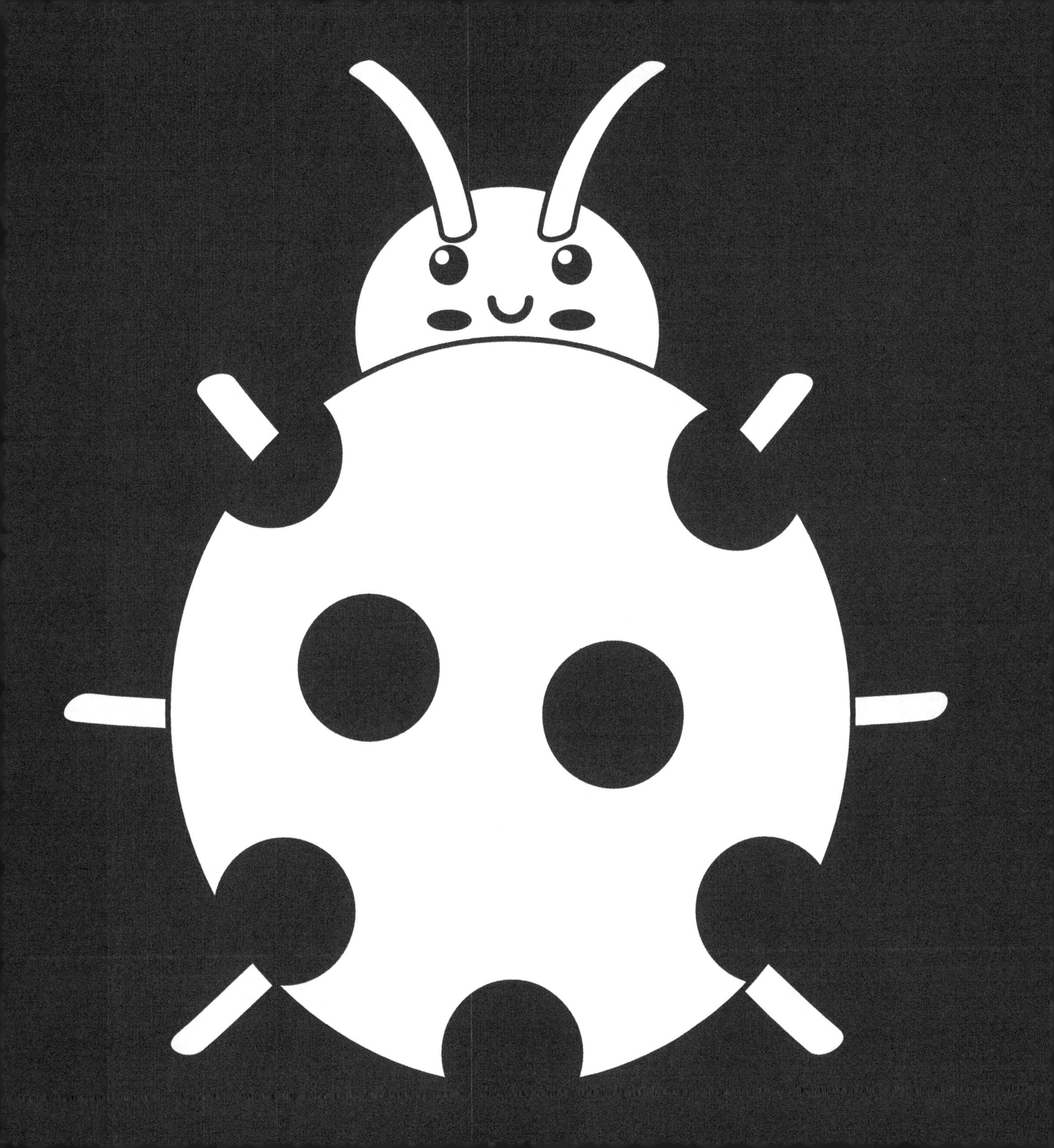

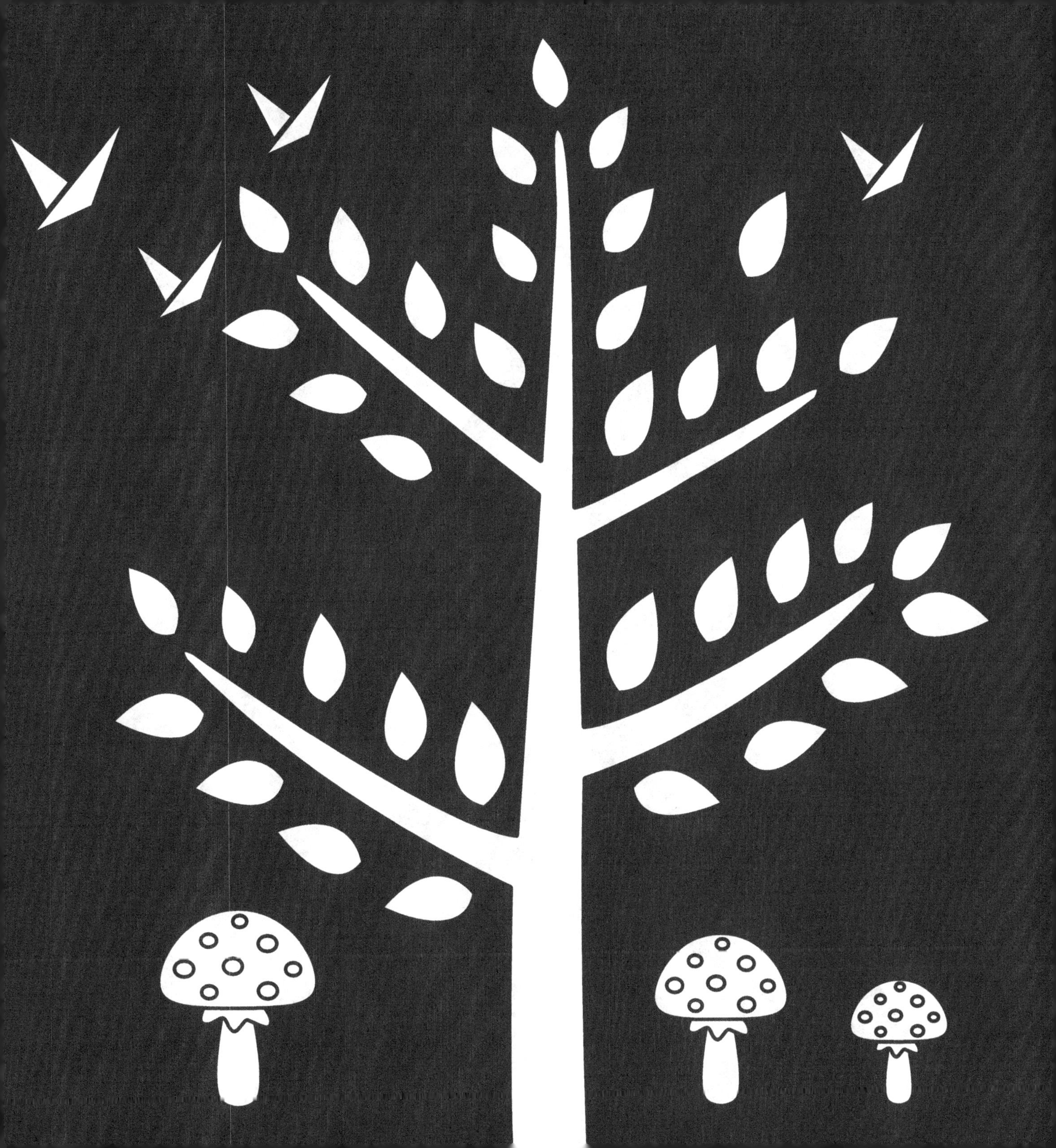

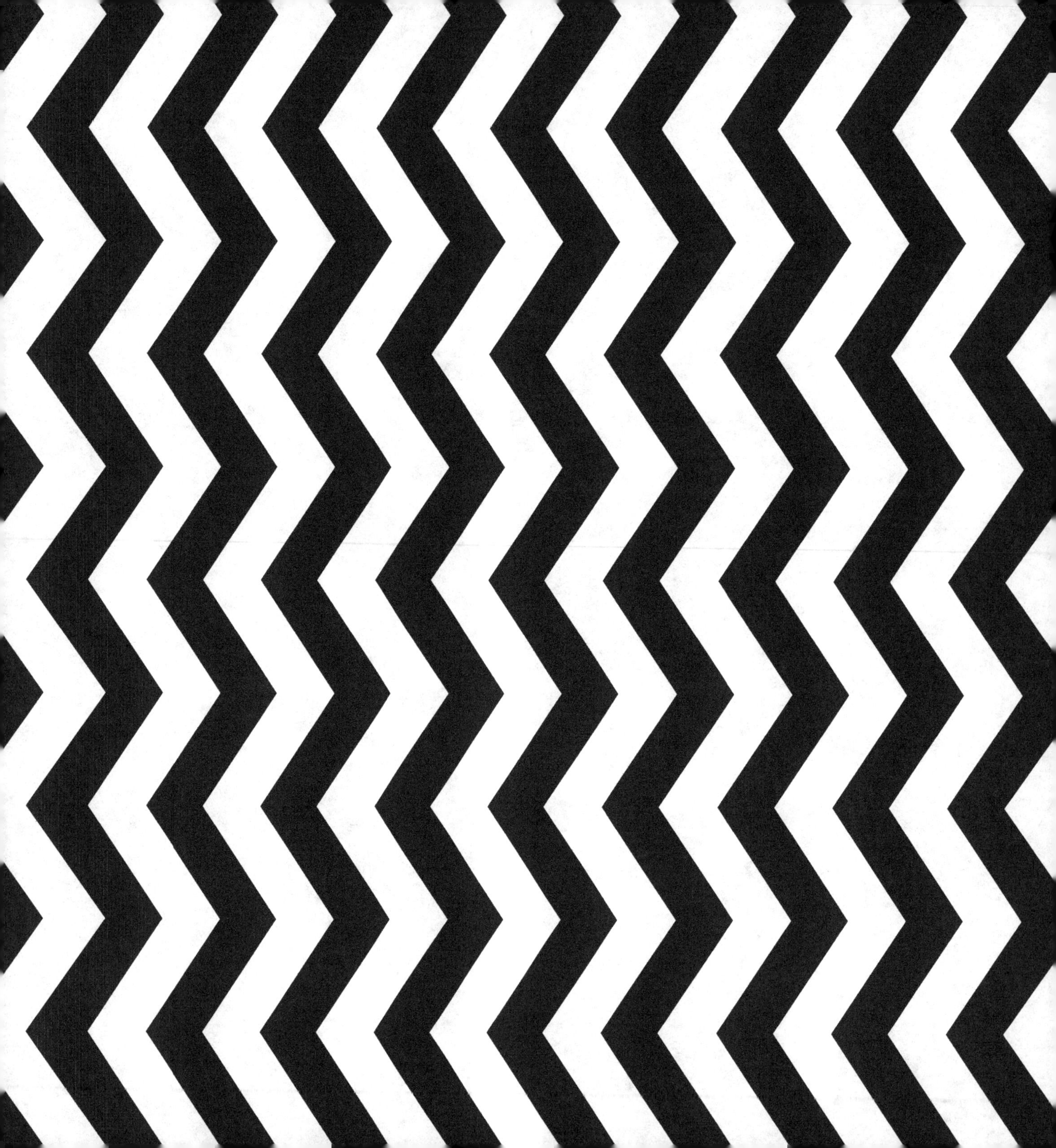

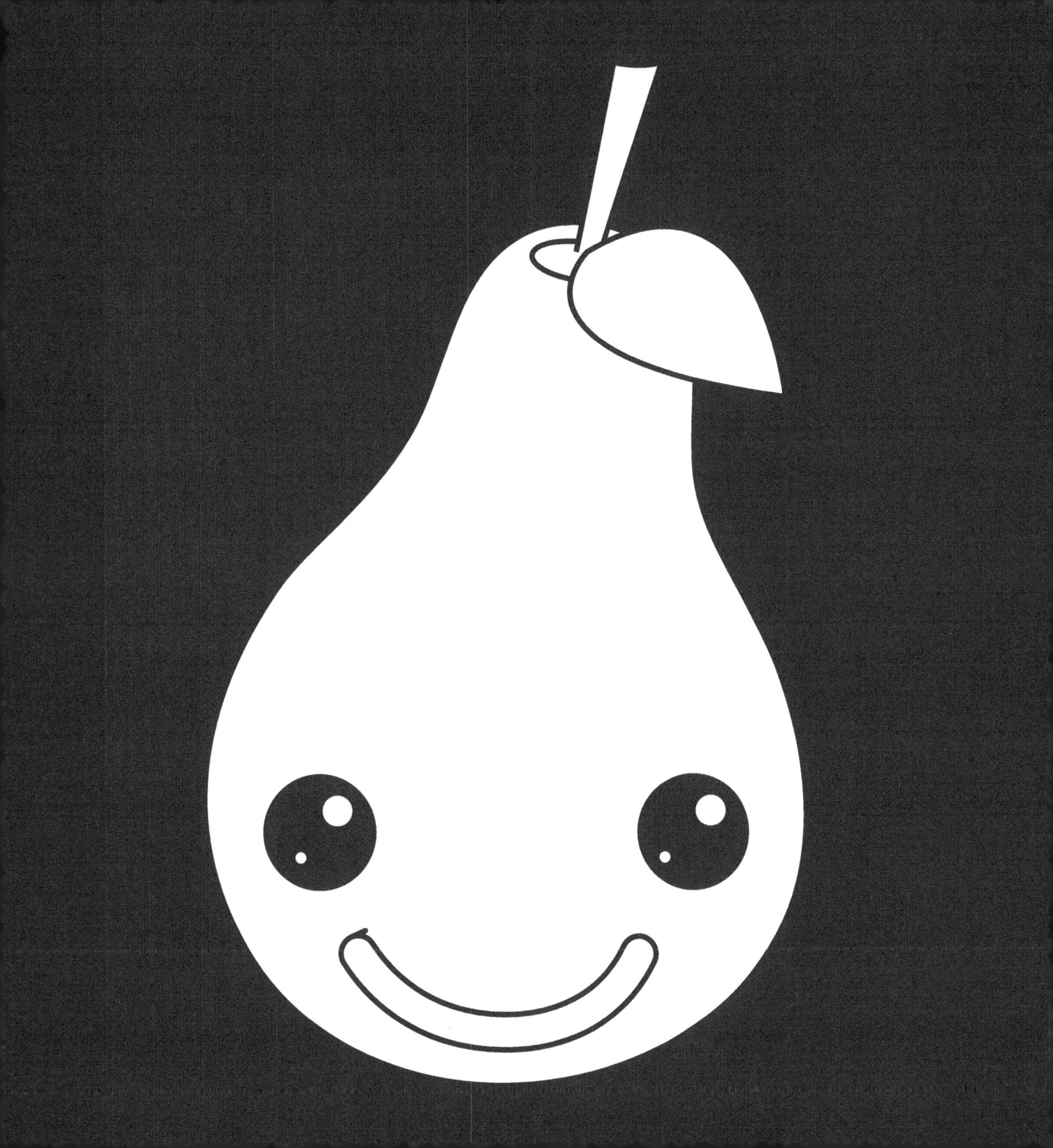

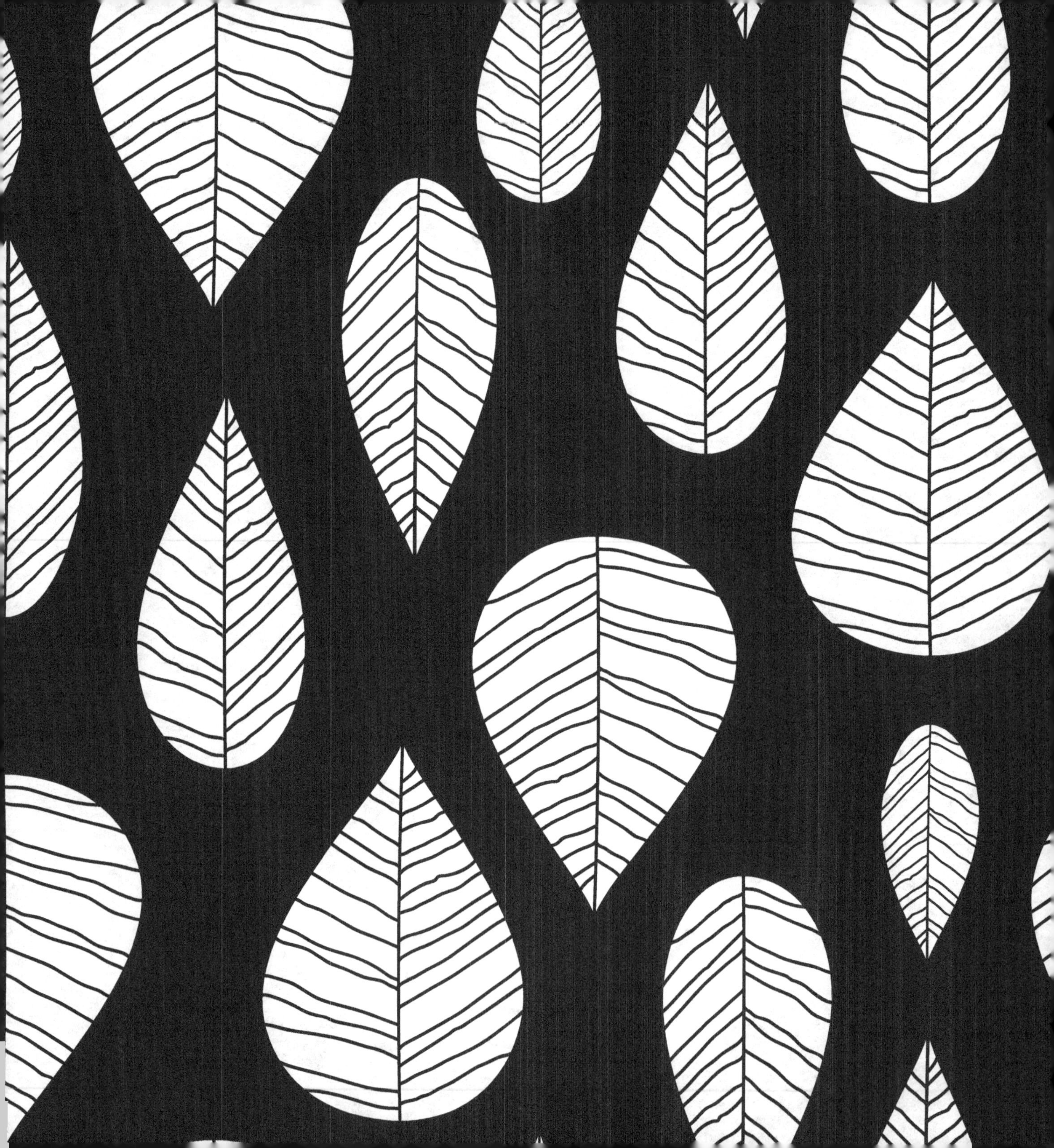

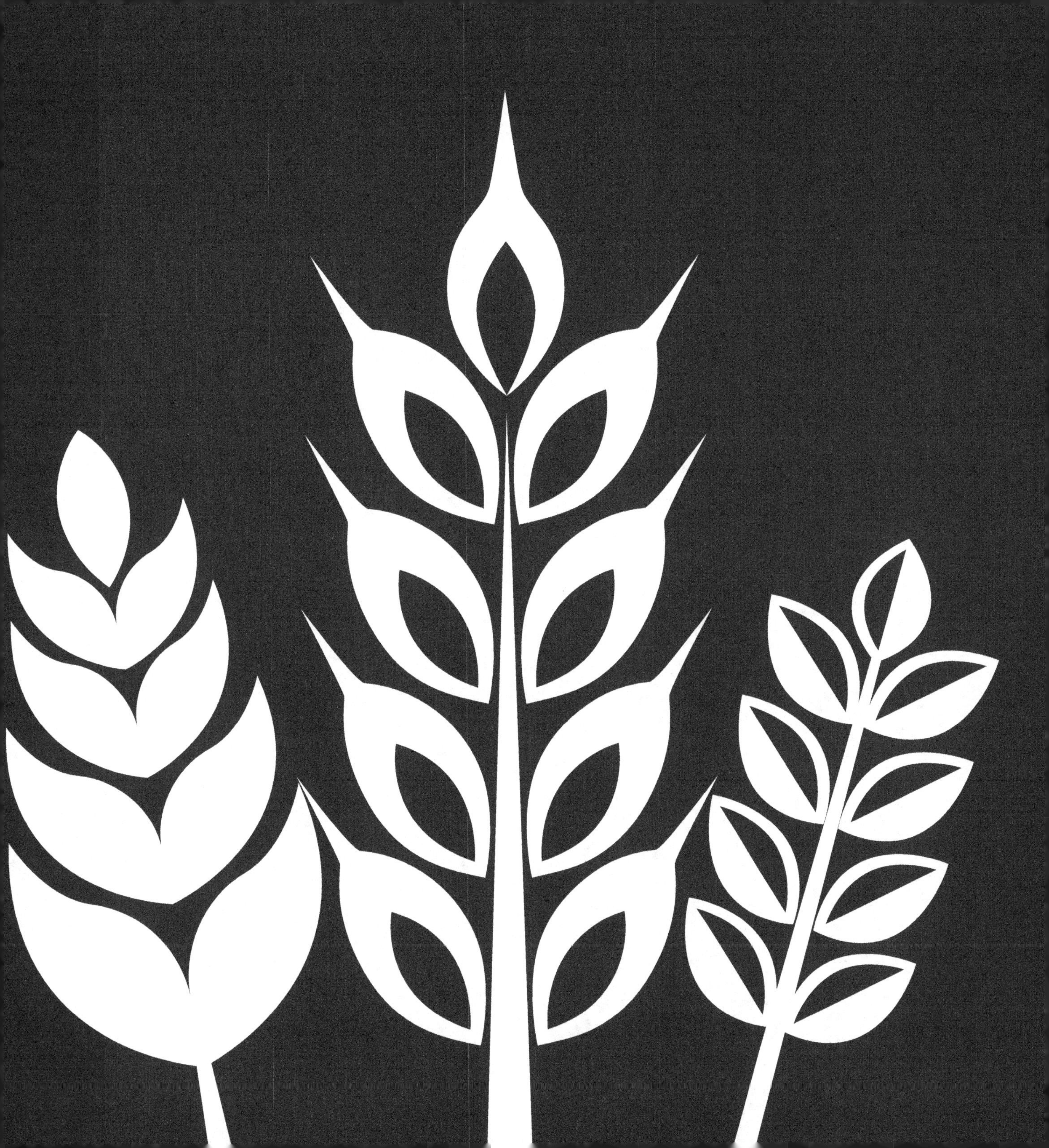

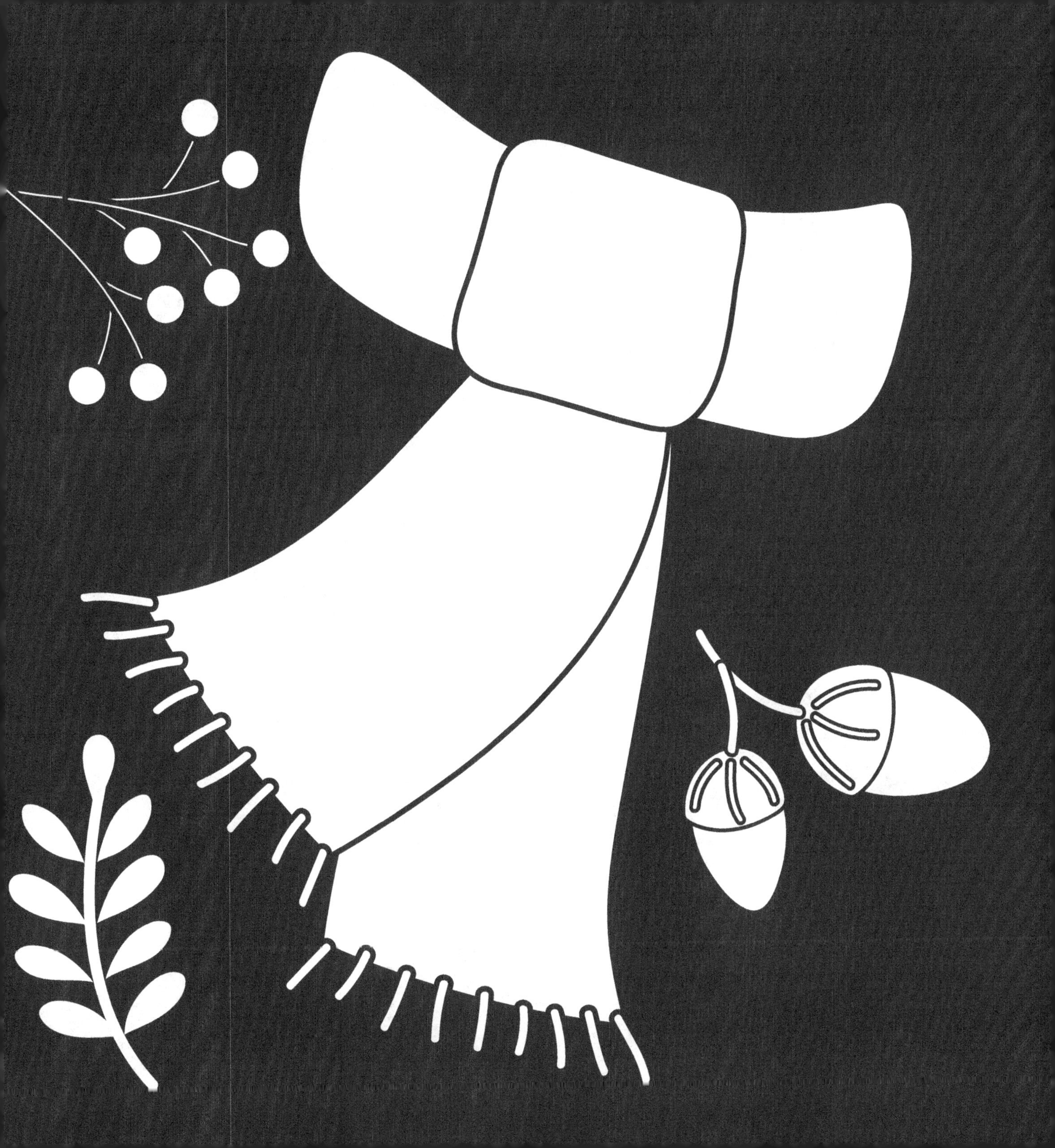

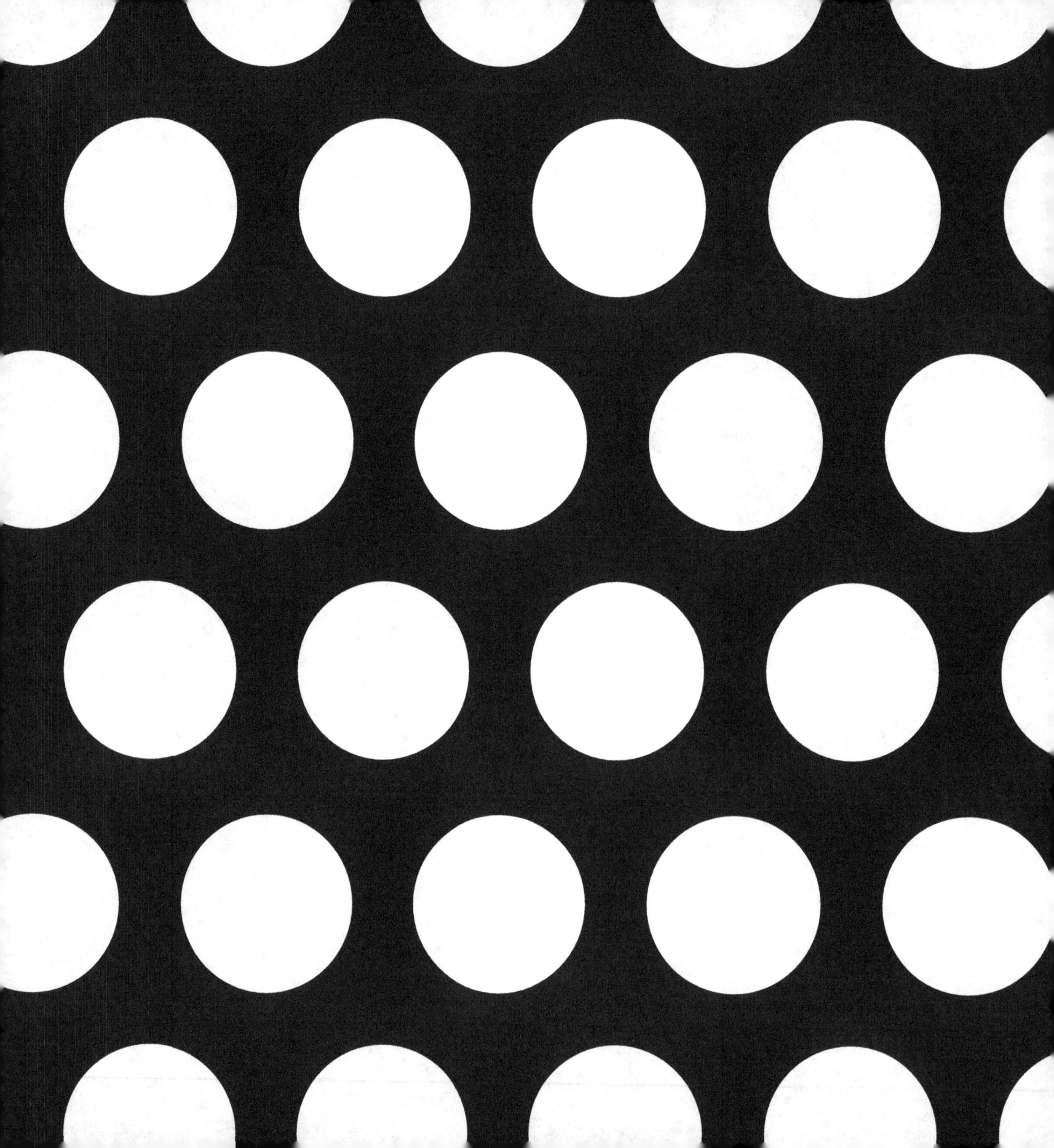

GO FOR IT!

Made in the USA
Monee, IL
12 October 2024

67703138R00024